ABOUT WRITING

A Field Guide for Aspiring Authors

Gareth L. Powell

Academia Lunare

LUNA PRESS PUBLISHING

ALSO BY GARETH L. POWELL

Novels:

Light Of Impossible Stars (2020)
Fleet Of Knives (2019)
Embers Of War (2018)
Ack-Ack Macaque: The Complete Trilogy (2017)
Macaque Attack (2015)
Hive Monkey (2014)
Ack-Ack Macaque (2013)
The Recollection (2011)
Silversands (2010)

Novellas:

Ragged Alice (2019)

Short Fiction Collections:

Entropic Angel (2017)
The Last Reef (2008)

ABOUT THE AUTHOR

Gareth L. Powell is an award-winning novelist specialising in science fiction and horror. He was born and raised in Bristol, UK, and was once fortunate enough to have Diana Wynne Jones critique one of his early short stories over coffee. Later, he went on to study creative writing under Helen Dunmore at the University of Glamorgan.

He is now a freelance creative writing tutor, and has run workshops and given guest lectures at several UK universities, including Aberystwyth, Bath Spa, Bucks New Uni, and York, as well as at the Arvon Foundation in Shropshire, and the Bristol and Stroud Literature Festivals.

In addition to his fiction, Gareth has written for The Guardian, The Irish Times, 2000 AD, and SFX. He has also written scripts for corporate training videos, and is currently at work on a screenplay.

He can be found online at: www.garethlpowell.com

First published by Luna Press Publishing, Edinburgh, 2019

www.lunapresspublishing.com
ISBN-13: 978-1-911143-59-8

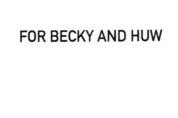

FOR BECKY AND HUW

Contents

Foreword

I have a friend I want to tell you about, because the chances are you might know someone just like him. You might even be someone just like him.

Now, I don't want to embarrass my friend, so for the purposes of this book, let's call him Bill. I see Bill maybe once a month at various literary events, and sometimes in the pub. Bill wants to be a novelist. He really, really wants to be one. And not just any novelist. No, Bill has convinced himself that he's going to write one of the great books of our time. After all, he spends all his time reading and criticising other books. He's seen just about every film made in the past thirty years, and he has an opinion on just about any writing-related subject you care to mention.

However, Bill never writes anything. Oh, he talks a good game. He's half-convinced everyone he knows that he's a serious author. He can tell you all about the book he's going to write. Like the character of Katin in Samuel Delany's novel *Nova*, he can rattle off half a dozen literary theories without pausing to draw breath, and without ever committing anything to paper. He never writes anything down for anyone else to read. Bill's convinced he has it in him to be a world-class novelist, but he's pushing fifty, working in a job he hates, and taking no active steps to achieve his dream.

Why?

Because Bill's expectations are too high. He's set his sights on writing a perfect novel without putting in the groundwork. He has so much of his self-image tied up in this idea of himself as a frustrated writer, a great talent waiting to be discovered, that if he ever actually finishes writing anything, and it isn't the shining masterpiece he sees himself as capable of producing, he'll be crushed.

So instead of writing, he makes excuses. He says he needs to find a physicist to check whether the physics of his idea are feasible; he says he needs to locate some obscure out-of-print book on sixteenth century witchcraft; and he says he can't possibly work unless he's alone with his muse for a month in a cottage on the edge of Dartmoor. These excuses are his security blanket. They are obstacles he puts in his own way, to avoid having to confront the fact that writing novels is hard, time-consuming work, and the only way to do it is to sit down and start typing. Better to feel that he could produce a brilliant book if only he could afford to take a month of work, than to just get on with it and be disappointed by the results. Better to cling to the comforting notion that he's an unrecognised genius than risk disappointing himself by failing to live up to all his talk.

Earlier, I used the phrase "without ever committing anything to paper", and that's the key: commitment. I like Bill as a person, and I think the ideas he has are terrific, and I wish he would write them instead of talking about them. But he never does. Like the overweight middle-aged guy who still dreams of being a professional footballer but never trains or tries out for a local team, Bill lacks the commitment to put in the hard work needed to achieve his goal.

If you want to write, you have to accept that the first draft you write will look pretty ragged. It will not be perfect. But the important thing is to get it written. That's the hard part. Once you actually have it all written down, it becomes real. It exists, and you can then take steps to polish and improve it. Expecting every word that flows from your fingers to be perfect first time is unrealistic and self-defeating, as you tend to get hung up endlessly trying to write the perfect first line, rather than ploughing ahead and telling the story.

I've spoken to a lot of writers who've told me that the first line, and sometimes even the whole first chapter, gets rewritten once the rest of the book is finished. So why waste your time trying to make it perfect, when the end of your book might suggest a different way for the story to open?

A couple of years ago, I wrote the following in reply to a question on my website, and I think the words are just as applicable to Bill (and all the other Bills out there). I wrote:

"I will give you the best piece of advice I was ever given: just write the fucking thing. Getting the words down on paper is the hard part. And it doesn't matter if your first draft sucks. All first drafts suck. The important part is that you write the story.

Then, when you've finished it, you can go back and edit it, polish up the text to make it shine. Editing is easier than writing. So, if you have a story to tell, just write it down without worrying how it sounds. You will not hit perfection first time. But you will get a completed first draft that you can then work on, to bring it up to professional quality. A lot of people make the mistake of trying to edit as they go along – of trying to make each sentence perfect before moving on to the next – and that is deadly. Just write. Tidy up later. Go for it."

And that's where this book comes in. I've been a professional writer for over a decade now; I've written ten novels and two collections of short stories, and I've learned a thing or two along the way.

There are a million books out there that will tell you about grammar and the importance of ditching adjectives. This isn't one of them. The pieces between these covers are despatches sent from the front lines: hard-won lessons from the last ten years. Things I wish someone had told me before I set out, and insights I've gleaned along the way.

I hope you find them helpful.

Especially you, Bill.

The Artist's Prayer

When in doubt, do the work.
When in obscurity,
When the rain falls and everything turns to ashes in
your hands,
When you are in love,
And when you are alone,
When the world clamours for your attention,
And when all have turned their backs upon you,
Do the work.

When tired, do the work.
When gripped by infirmity
Or paralysed by fear,
In the company of friends,
In ecstasy or desolation,
During the dark times and the light,
In anger and with compassion,
Do the work.

Part One

Getting Started

Advice For Young People

Many years ago, on a sunny day in 1993, I graduated from University of Glamorgan. I wore a mortarboard and gown, and climbed up on stage to receive my BA (hons) in Humanities. I was twenty-two years old at the time, and I didn't know what I wanted to do with the rest of my life. Actually, that's not strictly true. I knew I wanted to be a writer, but I had no idea how to go about it, and no expectation I'd be able to make a living from the angsty poems and overly-melodramatic short stories I'd been churning out for the creative writing classes I'd taken as part of my degree.

Being a writer, I thought, was something that happened to other people.

As a result, I spent the rest of my twenties in a series of dead-end call centre jobs, and I didn't really get my ass into gear and start writing seriously until I reached my thirtieth birthday, and realised it was time to stop talking about being a writer, and actually write something.

My first novel was published ten years later.

Writing is not a career for those who crave instant gratification!

Since that first novel, I've written eight more, plus a multitude of short stories. But I feel I left things a bit late. I could have written a lot more if I'd knuckled down when I left university, rather than letting everything drift for so many years.

So, that's my advice to you. If you have a dream – if you want to be a writer, artist, singer, actor or whatever – don't wait. Don't waste the next ten years promising you'll get around to your dream once you've established yourself in a more respectable career. Life passes far more quickly than you expect. Don't wither on the vine. Go out there and grab the world by the throat.

If you want to be a writer, declare to the world that you are a writer. Start thinking as a writer would think. React to situations the way a writer would. The only way to achieve your dream is to live it. Do what you have to in order to earn money, but don't let it define you. If you get a job in a bank, don't think of yourself as a banker who writes on the side, think of yourself as a writer who is a banker on the side. Dedicate yourself to your craft, and do one thing every day to bring success one-step closer.

Read and memorise The Artist's Prayer.

Trust me, the next ten years are going to pass at an incredible rate. Make the most of them.

My top tip for beginning
writers is to read,
read, read!

And when you're reading,
think about how the writer
creates mood and character.
How they use language.

Internalise the identity

I dislike the term "aspiring writer". You see it a lot in people's social media profiles, but to me it seems noncommittal. Either you write, or you don't. And if you do, please have the guts to say so. If you want to be a writer, don't wait to be asked.

Nobody's going to say, "Hey kid, would you like to be a writer?" You have to become one all by yourself. Start thinking and acting like one. Say to yourself, "I will look at the world the way a writer looks at the world. I will react to things the way a writer would react. When people ask me what I do, I will tell them I'm a writer. And when it is time to write, I will write like a writer." Life's too short to fuck about wasting time. Internalise the identity.

Next, convince yourself you can write, and then be confident enough to get some words on paper. And if your first attempts suck (and they probably will), have the balls to stick with it: keep learning, keep refining, and keep improving. There are no short cuts; you have to sit down and do the work. You have to have the confidence to produce a finished manuscript, and the humility to take criticism from readers, agents and editors. You have to be arrogant enough to believe that the world wants to hear what you have to say; but if you're too arrogant, nobody will want to work with you. Believe in yourself, but not to the exclusion of all else. Believe that you are a professional writer, and act like one. And what do professional writers do? They write. They put the work in. They strive to improve, to make every story they write better than the one they wrote before.

Aspiring writer? I'm an aspiring millionaire, but that doesn't mean I'll ever be one. Take yourself seriously. You might be unpublished, but if you believe in your heart that you're a writer, say so. Declare to the world that that is what you are, and act like it. Don't wait to be asked. Find your calling. Find a way to make it work. You won't get a second chance.

Everything I've achieved has been achieved by stepping outside my comfort zone and saying yes to things.

I wasn't sure I could do until I did them.

Where Do You Get Your Crazy Ideas?

It's a question all writers get asked, but few can honestly answer. We tend to use humour to dodge the issue. For instance, science fiction author Eric Brown swears there's a little old lady from Leeds who will, if you send her five pounds, mail you an idea by return of post. Neil Gaiman has spoken of a "little ideas shop in Bognor Regis." And, when readers ask how I came up with the idea to write a trilogy about a Spitfire-flying, cigar-smoking monkey, I tend to jokingly place the blame on alcohol and lack of sleep.

The truth though, as you've probably already realised, is a lot more complicated.

Ideas, you see, are rarely the problem. You can sit down with a sheet of A4 paper and jot down half a dozen while having your morning cup of tea. In fact, that's exactly what I've just done. Here are my six ideas from this morning's cuppa:

1. What would happen if everybody in the world suddenly forgot how to speak?
2. *Romeo & Juliet* set in modern day China.
3. The last woman on Earth writes a letter to her Martian daughter.
4. An ordinary housewife decides to become a super-villain.

5. A sentient comet composes haikus while falling towards the sun.
6. The world heavyweight-boxing champion turns out to be an android in disguise.

Now, I'm not claiming any of those are particularly good or original ideas, but each could certainly provide the seed for a longer story, and that entire list only took me three or four minutes to compose. Generating ideas is the easy part. The difficulty we face as writers is in finding the one particular notion that inspires us to take up our pens and start to write.

And often, it's not simply *one* idea. Sometimes, you need to smash two or more concepts together in order to generate a creative reaction. Look at John Wyndham's *Day Of The Triffids*, for example. In that story, he has the idea of the mobile, stinging plants. Unfortunately, by themselves they're not too scary. They are slow and vulnerable. But when he brings in his second idea, and introduces a cosmic meteor shower that blinds everybody on the planet, suddenly those plants become much more threatening, and that story becomes way more interesting.

In my experience, ideas for novels rarely arrive fully formed and ready to write. More often than not, the elements accrete over time like the ingredients of stars, slowly coalescing until they achieve a critical mass and spark into life.

These elements tend to surface while I'm in the shower or taking a walk. Sometimes they appear in that liminal haze between sleeping and waking, when the brain's still whirring away and you're not entirely sure whether or not you're still dreaming...

But where do these elements come *from*? That's what readers and aspiring writers want to know when they enquire as to where we get our ideas. They keep asking the question as if hoping we'll tell them that there's a special incantation or rite they can use to summon inspiration from the ether. But the fact of the matter is, these ideas come from *everywhere*.

When I was a child, my father had a shed, which he filled with things he found. There were green glass fishing net floats, lengths of rope, and pieces of driftwood found washed up on the beach; old fashioned ceramic bottles and pieces of pottery dug from the allotment; fossils; off-cuts of wood; old tools; a roof rack for a car we no longer owned; pots of paint; old doors and window frames; old metal signs... He liked collecting interesting bits of old junk because he thought they just might, one day, come in useful.

For me, my notebook is my shed. If I come across an interesting idea or unusual nugget of information, I'll jot it down and file it away. It doesn't matter what it is, if it stimulates my imagination, it gets saved somewhere.

For instance, way back in 2007, I stumbled across an article in *The Guardian*, revealing how Great Britain and France had almost formed a political union in the 1950s. At the time, I had no immediate use for that piece of information, but it caught my imagination and so I filed it away. I knew it would come in useful and sure enough, five years later, while I was searching for an alternate world in which to set the book that became *Ack-Ack Macaque*, it did. As did snippets I found about the remains of a great river delta that once lay under what is now the English Channel, and a TV documentary about a strip of once-inhabited land that now lies submerged beneath the North Sea.

The spaceship in the book I'm writing at the moment owes its distinctive shape to an old bullet I once saw in a dim and dusty military antiques shop, and its interior décor to a Royal Naval ship I once toured as a child.

Stories often arise from the collision of two unrelated ideas. Keeping a file of them, and looking back through it in search of inspiration, can suggest interesting juxtapositions and connections I might not otherwise have considered.

The same goes for old story ideas, snatches of conversation, and quick, two-or-three line observations of people, places and objects. They all go in the mixing pot because, as my father said, you never know when something might come in handy. What looks like trivia today might one day turn out to be exactly the inspiration you need. But, until that day, it'll bide its time quite happily in your notebook, disguised as useless old junk, just waiting for its moment to strike.

You'll be swimming lengths of the local pool, or walking the dog down by the canal, and lightning will strike. Your brain will make a new and unexpected connection between two hitherto unrelated concepts, and ask itself a question it's never asked before.

For John Wyndham, that moment came when he saw

a bramble bush blowing in the wind, and wondered what would happen if plants could move by themselves. For me, it came when I realised the best way to explore my questions about what makes us human would be through the eyes of an artificially sentient monkey.

It's difficult to force these sudden insights, but you can encourage them. In order to give your unconsciousness time to process all the cool oddments you've squirrelled away, you can distract yourself by taking a walk or a long, hot bath. And you can increase your chances of making new connections by providing your brain with as much raw material as possible.

- Open yourself to new experiences.
- Watch dramas and documentaries on all sorts of subjects.
- Read widely, both with and beyond the confines of your chosen genre.
- Learn new things, and meet lots of new people.

Try to live a life worth writing about, and the ideas will take care of themselves.

Don't wait for inspiration; just keep throwing ideas together until something sticks. Novels are like stars: their ingredients gradually clump together over time, until they achieve a critical mass and spark into life.

Finding Ideas: 55 steps to success

Okay, so you want to write a book. But what's it going to be about? Here's a quick tip to get your creative muscles warmed-up.

Open a spreadsheet (or use a Sharpie and a roll of paper, whatever works for you), and write the numbers one to fifty-five in the first column. Done that? Okay, now the fun starts.

We're going to write one idea for every one of those fifty-five numbers. It doesn't matter how good they are. This isn't the time to be critical. This is the time to be creative.

Start with number one and write the first thing that comes into your mind. I like to frame these as "What if?" questions, but you can use whatever format you prefer. So for me, the first few ideas might be,

What if cats developed telepathy?
What if grass became poisonous?
What if a ghost found itself haunted by a living person?
What if sand had an agenda?
What if everybody in the world suddenly developed the ability to travel in time?

As you can see, some of those are fairly random. But we're not here to judge. The purpose here is to fill those remaining fifty slots with the most off-the-wall creative ideas we can come up with. Only when we've done that will we go back and see if any of them start to suggest stories.

And if one suggests a partial story, try mixing it with another off the list. Sometimes you have to smash two story ideas together to achieve a critical mass.

Using my list above, imagine a story about a telepathic cat who helps a ghost that feels haunted by a living person. Or a world in which everybody could travel in time, but the food chain had crashed because grass had become poisonous.

Not all of your fifty-five ideas will be good, but some will be workable, or at least suggest interesting possibilities when smashed together with other ideas from the list. At worst, you will have spent fifteen minutes clearing some of the crap out of your brain, leaving you free to come up with even better ideas next time around...

Writing is the act of collapsing the phase space potential of the blank paper sheet down to a single narrative.
When you start writing, the wave function collapses and you have to stop dealing with potential stories and concentrate on the one at hand.

55 Story Ideas

A while ago, I started posting story ideas on Twitter each day, using the hashtag #DailyStoryIdeas.

If you're looking for inspiration, I've gathered together fifty-five of the best of those ideas into one post. Feel free to use and adapt them.

And if one of these ideas forms the seed for a bestseller, you can always buy me a drink sometime.

1. Aliens come to Earth, but mistake the Internet for the planet's dominant life form.
2. Twelve strangers wake up with a single letter tattooed on their bodies. They must seek each other out to read the message.
3. When an outspoken critic is murdered, the list of suspects includes some of the world's bestselling mystery writers.
4. For years, the queen has been playing the piano in memory of her lost love. When she stops, the world will end.
5. A psychic pawnbroker picks up "memories" from objects. A pawned gun leads him to the man who shot his wife.
6. A detective investigates the person who murdered him in a past life.
7. A murderer has hidden the name of his next

victim in the first letter of a series of tweets. But which account has he used?

8. A police SWAT team falls through a temporal rift into the power vacuum of post Roman Britain.

9. A guy develops superheroic powers, but can only use them in the presence of his five-year-old daughter.

10. A paddleboat is sinking in the Mississippi, but the card players won't leave their table until they've played the final hand.

11. A stranger appears at a Travel Lodge outside Milton Keynes. He is Odin, king of the Norse Gods. And he brings a message.

12. A hooligan scientist invents a device that lets him cross between parallel worlds, stealing the best inventions from each.

13. New letters start appearing in the alphabet, but no one knows where they came from. After a while, people start using them.

14. Locals say a ghost train haunts the line. One day, it pulls up at the station and all the ghosts get off.

15. A movie star becomes obsessed with a fan. Starts stalking them. No one will believe the fan. In desperation, they lash out.

16. Creatures live beneath the soft mud of the estuary. They pull unwary fishermen to their deaths. The locals call them trolls.

17. Zeus wearied of his duties and came to Earth. If you know where to look, you can find him running a junk shop in Brooklyn.

18. A golden door appears on the arctic tundra. From within can be heard the distant tolling of a cathedral bell. Who will enter?

19. Well-meaning time travellers prevent the Titanic disaster. What are the implications to history?

20. In the future, emotionless algorithms will decide who gets sent to labour camps. But algorithms can be hacked.

21. A party of werewolves searching for spiritual understanding in India run afoul of a pack of ravenous Bengal were-tigers.

22. There is a message hidden in the cosmic background radiation. It is the reboot code for the universe.

23. What if all moths are bio-engineered camera platforms sent back in time by future historians?

24. Wolves and coyotes howl because they alone know the true nature of the world.

25. Every time a woman goes to sleep, she wakes up the next morning in a different parallel universe. Never the same one twice.

26. A man trying to get home in the aftermath of an apocalypse steals a mobile library. Lends out books in return for food.

27. After a storm at sea, a modern day cruise liner returns to port to find it has somehow travelled to the eighteenth century.

28. An ageing writer and an upstart young critic meet on a hotel balcony overlooking the sea. One is pushed to their death.

29. Overnight, everyone on Earth develops the ability to read each other's thoughts. Every lie is revealed, every relationship.
30. A child finds a sword made from scorpions and fire, and a shield fashioned from poetry and ice.
31. Magic is dangerously real, but only toddlers can wield it. The ability fades at age five, as reason takes over the brain.
32. The birds believe their singing causes the sun to rise. Turns out they're right.
33. A woman lives in a shack on the beach, waiting for the tide to wash up usable fragments from the distant apocalypse.
34. The sun becomes sentient. Humanity tries to teach it how to communicate. Then other stars start to wake up.
35. Inside an old castle that's more ivy than stone lies a princess whose nightmares become flesh and prey on the townspeople.
36. An AI engraves its memories in seven gemstones. When the stones are scattered, it hires a faun to find them.
37. Humanity finds itself as just another set of counters in an intricate war game played by pan-dimensional centaurs.
38. Two friends joke that if neither has married by the age of 40, they'll marry each other. Many years later, they meet in a cafe.
39. A comic book artist decides to become the superhero he has spent the last ten years drawing.

40. A woman lives alone on a beach. At night, the sea whispers stories. It tells her of other survivors in other lands.
41. The world looks up to find a message of dire portent written on the face of the full moon. In ancient Sanskrit.
42. A hunting party turns lethal when the rich hunters find themselves attacked by a pack of disturbingly cunning hyenas.
43. The crack of fireworks. Sparks leap from the bonfire. In the darkness, a secret is whispered.
44. The eclipse has lasted a thousand years. Now it draws to an end. The night creatures must cede the land to the humans.
45. Jumping through hyperspace is dangerous. One often emerges with a different personality. Sometimes a whole new identity.
46. A man contracts temporal narcolepsy. Every time he falls asleep, he wakes up a random number of years further into the future.
47. Escaped nanotech starts reshaping the Pacific garbage patch into something hideously alien. And alive.
48. A house becomes infatuated with the family that lives in it. It protects them. It serves them. It won't let them leave.
49. Trapped on an island when civilisation falls, a lighthouse keeper struggles to survive. Then a boat washes up on the beach.
50. A detective is visited by his time-travelling older

self, who warns him to stop investigating his brother's murder.

51. A palaeontologist finds a dinosaur fossil wearing what appears to be a leather belt and a knife carved from a t-rex tooth.

52. A hive of bees becomes sentient and embarks on a campaign of revenge against those poisoning the land.

53. Crooked cop blackmails hacker to find drug money. Drug dealer kills cop. Hacker kills drug dealer. Hacker takes money.

54. When a market town expands, the gods of city and countryside go to war with one another over the disputed territory.

55. A person gains the ability to change appearance at will, but forgets their true identity.

Many authors list their agents on their social media bios. If you're searching for an agent, take a peek at your favourite authors' Twitter or Facebook profiles.

Choosing Your Twitter Teachers

One of Twitter's most useful features is the ability to create lists. Using them, you can cut through the maelstrom and focus on the people you really want to follow.

As an author, I have a variety of lists (some public, some private) that I use on a daily basis. These include selections dedicated to book news, publishers, other authors, and so on. I even have one called *Local Emergency*, which draws together all the police, fire and local news feeds in case I need a quick update on an unfolding situation.

But the one I want to talk about now is the private list I have called *Teachers*.

(Private means only I can see it).

This list isn't huge. There are around twenty people on there. But these twenty people are some of the most successful and talented authors on the planet. And I've chosen them because I want to learn from them. I want to see what they're talking about, what they're retweeting. Find out what's important to them.

Even though they don't know it, these people are my mentors. Scrolling through the list is like standing in a hotel bar, listening to them all talking. It's like the world's best ever convention, or a university seminar where I've selected the guest speakers.

If I'm going to learn, why not learn from the best?

Who would you put on your list? Who are the people

you want to learn from, or aspire to emulate? Why not take ten minutes and choose your own list of Twitter teachers?

> If you have a dream, don't wait. Start working towards it now.
> Do one thing every day to bring that dream closer to reality.

Getting started

Sitting down to write a novel can be a nerve-wracking experience. That first page is one of the biggest hurdles you're going to face. All that blank white space looks terrifying. You have an idea of what you want to write in your head, but where do you start? *How* do you start?

I thought I'd share a little trick with you that I use to get myself going when I'm about to start a new book.

Before going to bed, I open up a Word document, format it as a novel manuscript, and I write a couple of hundred words. I don't think about them, I just write them down as quickly as I can. A character arrives on a beach with a mysterious bundle, asking to see another character. Boom. No stopping, pausing or editing; no worries about quality or sense. I write them and then I go to bed, knowing that when I sit down to work in the morning, I won't be facing the potentially soul destroying emptiness of a blank page. I'll have a place to start. Even if I end up deleting most of the words written, I'd at least be doing something.

And, I'm pleased to tell you that it works. I get up feeling as if I've already made a start on the book. I am over that first hurdle and my mind is working away on the rest of the chapter. By the time I sit at my desk, I am ready to carry on with the story. I don't bother editing or rewriting the paragraphs I wrote the night before, as they generally turn out to be quite serviceable, and I know that I'll be going back to edit them later on. Right now, the important thing is to press on and get the rest of the story written. I'm not going to obsess over the opening sentence, striving for perfection, as events later in the book might cause me to have to come back and totally change this opening scene. For now, I'm going to leave it the way it is and carry on writing. There'll be plenty of time for editing later.

Sometimes it's difficult to choose between story ideas.

Ask yourself, "If I only had six months to live, which would I want to write?"

How to keep being creative in a crisis

As writers or artists, we're often preoccupied with our work. But sometimes, real world events intrude and leave us feeling unable to summon the energy to be creative, or leave us questioning the value of art in the face of tragedy.

When there's a disaster or an unfolding crisis on the news, it can sometimes paralyse us. *Why am I writing books about spaceships or painting pictures of abstract nudes*, you might think, *when there's been an appalling disaster or terrorist attack, or when the economy's tanking and the threat of global warming seems so pressing and bleak? How can art possibly matter in such a world? What's the point?*

How do we, in short, keep functioning in a crisis?

When I start to feel that way, I think back to everything writers and artists have had to contend with in the past. Our Palaeolithic ancestors daubed handprints on the walls of their caves, and carved figures from stone and wood. The Vikings told their sagas. Even as Rome fell, there were poets writing and sculptors sculpting. In the Dark Ages, people were still singing songs and telling folk tales. Poets wrote in the trenches of WWI. While the Cuban Missile Crisis raged, people were still reading and writing novels and short stories. In 1984, at the height of the Cold War, with nuclear obliteration seemingly imminent, movies and TV programmes were made and watched, books were written and paintings painted and sold.

Art doesn't stop for history. In some ways, art is history. It's the way we record how we feel about our present, and a window on the thoughts and feelings of the past. And it's also one of the best means we have to influence the future.

The language of a civilisation determines its development. If that language is one of fear and exclusion, oppression and hatred, the phrases and concepts those words encapsulate become ingrained in the fabric of everyday thought. They become normalised, and therefore more readily accepted. But if the language employed is one that favours tolerance and empathy, it can be those qualities that come to the fore.

Art and fiction are important because they put us in the shoes of others. They create empathy and understanding, and promote education and intelligence. They allow us to share ideas and discuss what it means to be human, and unpack the fundamental commonalities we all share. They can reveal truths, expand our minds, and provide lifetimes of enjoyment. But most of all, they encourage us to dream of other, better worlds, and begin to imagine how we might reach them.

No single painting or novel can change the world, just as no single drop of rain can wash away a town. We may feel we have no control over global events. But culture is a cumulative phenomenon, and every drop helps create the flood.

We all need a little escapism sometimes. Life would be a drudge were we unable to escape into fantasy worlds now and again, and there's nothing frivolous about providing readers with fictional boltholes. Indeed, it's a vital role that bards have been playing right back into the dawn of prehistory.

As artists and writers, our work allows us to express what's in our minds and hearts. As consumers, it can comfort and distract us; but it can also educate and inspire, and nourish our souls. If we ever lost our art and fiction – or simply gave up producing them – we'd have lost a fundamental part of ourselves, and be all the poorer for it.

Art is one of the candles of civilisation. If we abandon it, the bad guys win.

So, pick up that paintbrush. Open that Word document. Every stroke of paint or line of prose you make is a blow struck against entropy and ignorance, and a contribution to the net beauty of the world. You are not being self-indulgent, you are *communicating* – and communicating is what people *do*. We're a social species, and we need you to help bring forth and express our shared inner lives. To add your voices to the chorus of those who have gone before, uncounted, into the darkness, and simply say to the universe, "WE ARE ALIVE!"

Employ a structure of
peaks and troughs that
continually build the
tension towards the finale.
Think of it as a piece of
music. The tempo falls and
rises and builds to
a final crescendo.

Beating Writer's Block With 100 Words

I don't have a daily target for the number of words I'm going to write. I'm happy if I manage 1000 on a good day. But on bad days, when I have no urge at all to write, I have a little trick I use to keep me moving forwards.

"Just write one hundred words," I tell myself. After all, a hundred words is easy. Typing double-spaced in Word, it's less than half a page.

When writing seems too daunting, writing a hundred words is doable. And sometimes, those hundred words will get me started, and I'll go on to write more.

But even if I stop after writing them, at least I've added a hundred words to the project. At least I'm still moving towards my goal.

So, how about it? Do you feel like writing a hundred words?

[*Thanks to my sister, Rebecca Powell, author of* The Brazilian Husband, *who introduced me to this idea.*]

I think sometimes you have to put a few miles on the clock before you can write about the journey.

How to write a novel outline

Some authors like to plot out the entire book in advance, so they know exactly what's going to happen in every chapter before they start writing. Others prefer to wing it, to let the characters guide the story, and make it up as they go along.

There are pros and cons to each approach.

The former can be useful if you need to write your novel quickly, as you know you won't get stuck because you have it all worked out in advance.

Paul Cornell, author of the Shadow Police series, says the outline he's working on for his next book currently stands at 15,000 words, and it's still not finished. "Basically," he jokes, "I just need to add 'he said' and 'she said'.

"I exaggerate," he continues. "It's 100 numbers, with a paragraph of described action for each. It's going to take a bit more work to fill in 1,000 words of prose for each of them!"

Author and comic writer, Cavan Scott takes a similar approach. "It all starts with my trusty journal," he says, "scribbling down notes, and more importantly questions: 'Why does the hero do this?', 'What would happen if that spaceship explodes?' and so on. These usually morph into mind-maps with ideas spider-webbing everywhere and sometimes even doodles.

"When I've worked out the general direction of the plot, I break everything down into scenes, using index cards. This used to be physical cards but now, more often than not, I use the virtual index cards in Scrivener on my Mac, or an Index Card app on my iPad. These get swapped around and sorted into the order that the story will run until I have an outline I can work from."

The downside of writing a detailed outline like this is that such a meticulous structure can feel constraining, with no room for creative digression. And if you take it too far, you can exhaust the storytelling impulse before you've actually started writing, leaving the book itself as an uninspiring exercise in joining-the-dots. For instance, an editor I know remembers the time an author handed in a 70,000-word outline for a 90,000 word book, and then had to somehow turn it into a novel!

Perhaps with this in mind, Stephen King recommends the latter approach in his book, On Writing. He likens stories to fossils that you have to unearth one painstaking sentence at a time. This gives the author total creative freedom to follow the story in whichever direction it wants to go, which can be great for writers who like to let their characters guide the flow of events, but it can lead to problems (and major rewrites) if you don't stay aware of pacing and dramatic structure.

For some people, a Post-it note will suffice. For others, half a dozen handwritten pages. Some plot each scene on an index card, so they can shuffle them around (something you can do electronically with software such as Scrivener), or just scribble the basic plot points on a napkin or cigarette packet.

Personally, I've written outlines in notebooks and Word documents, on scrap pieces of paper, and even once on the inside of an opened-out takeaway pizza box.

With my "Macaque" novels, my outlines were two or three pages outlining the basic events of the novel. "They go to the parallel world, grab the Zeppelin and return."

For one particular outline, I went into more detail. The book I wanted to write was a thriller taking place in a confined space (sort of like the movies Speed or Phone Booth), and so the plot needed to be worked out before I started. I needed to know how the main character was going to survive and fight back before I started, otherwise there was the danger I might accidentally paint him (and myself) into an inescapably tight corner.

In order to do this, I started with an Excel spread sheet. I created two columns. In the first, I wrote the numbers 1 to 50. These were my chapter numbers. In the second column, I wrote a paragraph about each chapter, describing the significant events. I told myself the story, starting at chapter one and working my way through to the end, jotting down these notes as I went.

Once I had it all written down, I began to see the structure. Certain events made more dramatic sense if they happened before others, and so I was able to switch the cells around until I had everything in the right place. It felt like editing a movie or TV show, swapping the order of the scenes around in order to build suspense. Then, when I was done, I pasted the whole thing into Word.

What I ended up with was a numbered list of 50 paragraphs, which between them broke down my story into significant events. And if I wrote 2,000 words for each of these fifty chapters, I'd end up with a 100,000 words.

I knew I wouldn't stick to this outline with total rigidity. New ideas would occur as I wrote, and characters would go off in unexpected directions. But this document formed the foundation on which the rest of the book could be built.

If you want an analogy, I see outlining as akin to planning a journey using a satellite photo. You can see the major landmarks and the general lie of the land, so you won't get lost. But, when you actually start walking, there's still plenty of scope to discover new and exciting details along the way.

And when I'm ready to submit the finished novel to my agent or publisher, that outline can (with some tinkering) form the basis of the synopsis I'll need to include with the manuscript.

The main thing to remember is that different authors prefer different approaches. Some like to plot in advance, others like to fly by the seat of their pants. It depends on the individual, and sometimes on the type of book they're trying to write, and it may take some experimenting before you discover which method works best for you.

Pay attention to your dreams. They are the place where your desires and fears run unchecked.

Dreams

I'm a big believer in the significance of dreams. Not in any supernatural way. Just in the way that they can help us understand our own feelings, see the world from fresh angles, and even resolve emotional issues.

For instance, since my father died, I've had several extremely vivid dreams about talking to him and discussing the afterlife and my feelings about his loss. These dreams were so vivid, I could almost believe they really happened – but I understand that they are really my own brain trying to resolve my feelings of grief by constructing a way for me to be able to tell him all the things I wish I could tell him in real life.

Similarly, I've had dreams about friends, where I hug them and tell them how much I miss them. It's a coping mechanism. And sometimes I'll have a dream that feels so real I want to ring up the people I was dreaming about and ask them if they were having the same dream, because it feels impossible that I wasn't actually talking to them.*

But the dreams I really pay attention to are the ones I can't immediately interpret. The ones that feel real but have no readily identifiable cause, or feature people who seem familiar, but whom I don't know in real life. These dreams come from somewhere else in my brain, and while they may be examining an emotional truth, they also engage the imagination and my narrative urges.

They are stories.

In some ways, writing has always felt like dreaming out loud.

And that's why I keep a notebook beside my bed – because I've taken inspiration for many works of fiction from these vivid dreams, and it's essential to jot down the salient points immediately upon waking, before the memories start to fade.

Anyway, this is all a longwinded way of telling you to make sure you have paper and pen within easy reach when you're asleep, because you never know when inspiration will strike, and there's nothing worse than trying to summon the willpower to leave a warm bed at 4am in order to go downstairs to make notes.

*If you ever have a dream like that about me, do drop me a line, just in case.

I usually have an ending in mind, and a few events along the way. Kind of like a sketch map. Everything else is made up as I go along, including the characters. I will have an idea who they are, but their personalities evolve on the page, as they talk and interact.

8 Steps To Becoming A Published Writer

I'm assuming you already know how to string a sentence together, so I'll skip the nitty gritty. (If you're not sure, there are plenty of good books on the subject. I recommend the *Oxford Style Manual*, or *The Elements of Style* by Strunk and White, but there are many others).

You may be slightly disappointed to learn that there are no shortcuts. Becoming a published writer is hard work – but if writing is what you love doing, then that hard work will be enjoyable in and of itself.

So, here, and without any further ado, are my **8 Steps To Becoming A Published Writer**.

1. **Write**. It doesn't matter when you write or how much you write, as long as you write. If you don't write, you're not a writer, the same way a skier who sits at home all day dreaming about the mountains instead of strapping a pair of skis to his feet isn't a skier.
2. **Read**. Read everything you can get your hands on. Read good books and bad books, and try to figure out what makes the good ones good and the bad ones bad. Look at the way dialogue is used to create character. Figure out what stories have already been told, and look for new ones – or at least, new spins on old themes.

3. **Observe**. Watch people. Listen to the way they talk and interact. Notice their mannerisms. Learn to pick out salient details. Nothing kills a story faster than flat, two-dimensional characters; so tune your ears to the way real people speak, and how they reveal themselves through their words and gestures.

4. **Finish**. Whatever you're writing, finish it. There are no two ways around this, no short cuts. Just as a carpenter can't sell a chair without legs, so you can't sell a half-written story. Sometimes, people ask what the secret is, and it is this: **finish**. Having a finished book is what distinguishes the writers from the wannabes. Loads of people want to write a novel, relatively few ever get to the end. But if you "want to be a writer", this is what you have to do.

5. **Accept that the first draft will be rough**. But that's okay. That's what first drafts are for. They give you a place to start. Don't get disheartened, but also, don't show anyone what you've got yet. First you have to...

6. **Edit. Rewrite. Revise**. Keep going back through your story, tightening up the plot and fixing the bits that simply don't work. Then, when you think you're done, ask a couple of trusted friends to read it. If they give you honest feedback, maybe you'll need to go back and do some more revision. The key thing is, you shouldn't send it out into the world until it is the very best that you can make it.

7. **Find an agent**. If you've written a novel, you'll
    need to find an agent. Do some research; find
    an agent who deals with the kind of story you've
    written and find out what their submissions
    policy is. Find authors you admire and find out
    who their agent is. Then submit your work. Keep
    repeating this stage until you find an agent willing
    to represent you, and who you're happy to have
    represent you. With luck, they'll sell your book
    for you.

Or...

*   **Submit your work to a small press.** There are
    many excellent and reputable small presses around.
    For instance, NewCon Press (which published
    my 2017 short story collection, Entropic Angel)
    is essentially a one-man operation, run by the
    inestimable Ian Whates, but regularly publishes
    works by respected authors, and its books can
    regularly be found on the shortlist for genre
    awards. Luna Press Publishing and Fox Spirit
    Books are two others currently putting out good
    work, and filling the niches larger publishers
    cannot.
*   **Self publish.** With the advent of ebooks, it's now
    possible to self publish your work online. This is
    fine, and some self-published authors have gone
    on to make a name for themselves. Equally, there
    are thousands, possibly millions who've remained

in obscurity. If you publish your own work, you have to be prepared to publicise it yourself; to get out there and let people know about it.

8. **Write something else.** Whatever happens, you have to start work on the next story. Remember what I said at the beginning? A writer writes. So, good luck, and keep writing!

Part Two

Writing

3 Ways To Breathe Life Into Your Fiction

New writers are often given the following piece of advice: "Write what you know". In other words, concentrate on the things you've observed and the things you understand about the world around you. If you're a former journalist wanting to write a mystery, make your main character a journalist; if you're a coal miner, write about the dangers and camaraderie of life down the pit.

Such first-hand experience can add verisimilitude to your fiction; but what happens if you're trying to write genre fiction? What if you're trying to write about a future society so far removed in time that they barely remember the present day? What if you're trying to write about a supernatural horror preying on a group of cave divers, or a lone warrior on a quest across a mythic fantasy kingdom? In science fiction, fantasy and horror, characters are routinely put in situations in which it would be impossible for the writer to gain any direct experience. How then can you convincingly fill in these scenes using only your imagination?

1. Identify the parts of the scene you *do* know.

People for example. Your characters should be recognisably human, each with their own distinct personalities and foibles. No matter how fantastical the situation, you can base your characters on your own experiences of people and the way they interact with one another.

Sometimes when writing fiction, it's hard to keep a consistent mental image of all the characters involved, and mistakes start to creep in. You get muddled and describe your hero as having blue eyes in chapter two and green ones in chapter six. To get around this problem, I suggest casting your story in the same way you'd cast a movie. Go through magazines and pick out photos of actors, celebrities, models, or "real" people to represent your characters, and stick them on the wall behind your computer monitor. Not only will this help you keep their physical descriptions consistent as you write, it'll also help you visualise your scenes better, and you may even find the pictures suggest things you can work into the story to give your characters added depth, such as facial tics, a preference for a particular style of clothes, or an unusual mannerism, such as a raised eyebrow or twisted smile.

2. Draw on incidents from your own life and try to map them onto the situations in which your characters find themselves.

I've never been involved in a gun battle, for instance, but I *have* been paintballing. I know what it's like to hunker down uncomfortably behind a tree stump with gravel digging into my knees, to run out of ammo at a crucial moment, and to take a high-velocity pellet to the stomach, head or leg.

It's easier to write about characters in extreme

situations if you've had a few adventures of your own. In my time, I've also flown a light aircraft; been punched in the face; crawled through potholes; kayaked down white water rapids; jumped off a bridge; taken fencing and shooting lessons; had my heart broken; swum in Loch Ness; and climbed a number of mountains. I know what it's like to be tired and wet and cold; I know what it's like to lose someone; and what it feels like to break a bone. Drawing on these experiences can add authenticity to the most fantastical situations, by providing the small details and observations that really bring a scene to life.

3. Know your setting.

In genre writing, it helps if you know your setting inside out. If it's the flight deck of a space shuttle, research all you can; find images online; try to find a simulator, or at least set foot on the flight deck of an airliner. If it's an invented city, then make sure you know everything there is to know about it. Visit London or Amsterdam or Barcelona and look at the old buildings. Use Google Maps to "walk" through the streets of cities in Japan, America and Europe. Get the flavour of as many cities as possible, and take the bits you like to furnish your creation. Draw maps. Immerse yourself to the point where you can see your city in your mind's eye and hear, smell, and feel its hustle and bustle around you.

As my first novel, Silversands, was set on a distant planet, I spent months assembling notes about the planet's climate, orbit, geography and seasons. I researched anaerobic bacteria, magnetic weaponry and weird terrestrial sea life. I got to know the characters, their back-stories and personalities. I even based the craggy landscape on my childhood memories of Pembrokeshire, with its plunging rocky cliffs and yellow-tipped gorse bushes. By the time I finished writing the novel, I had an entire box full of background notes, sketches and maps. Most of that information didn't make it into the finished story, but it played a vital part in helping me convincingly visualise and communicate the setting.

Of course, I'm not downplaying the importance of imagination. A strong imagination is one of the genre writer's most essential tools, and without it, you may as well be writing nonfiction. In order to write genre fiction, you need the audacity to make bold leaps into the unknown and turn the everyday world on its head. My argument is that if you want to lend authenticity to your flights of fancy, you need to do your research, observe the people around you, and have your own adventures.

**Ask yourself:
Does this scene/chapter move the plot along? If not, it's probably not relevant, and can be cut.**

Ten Tips For Novelists

1. Never tell anyone your idea until you've written the first draft, otherwise you'll lose the storytelling impetus.
2. Don't waste time trying to write the perfect opening sentence. Chances are you'll have to change it later anyway.
3. Write first, edit later.
4. Break the story into a series of important events or revelations. Each event or revelation gets a scene.
5. Finish what you start. You can't tell if it's any good, or edit it to make it so, until it's finished.
6. Only send out your best work.
7. Accept that the first draft will be rough.
8. Avoid exhausting descriptive passages by using small details to suggest the bigger picture.
9. Bring scenes to life by making use of all the senses. What do your characters see, smell, taste, and touch?
10. Listen to the way people talk. Notice their mannerisms. Flat, two-dimensional characters can kill a story.

Bonus:

11. Feel free to disregard all advice. What matters is your story.
12. Don't let good reviews go to your head; don't let bad reviews go to your heart.

You have to get into your characters' heads. This means all of them have a part of you in them. I imagine them talking as if I am acting out their parts for them.

Five Essential Rules For Writing
Better Fiction

Writing is an activity with many rules. Some are imposed upon the writer by the conventions of spelling and grammar; others are self-imposed, and arise from observation and experience. The rules below fall into this latter category, and I try to keep them in mind whenever I'm working on a new composition.

1) Write as clearly as you can. Don't give your readers a hard time with obscure or unpronounceable words, vague descriptions and convoluted sentences. Say what you mean to say, and give the readers enough information for them to picture the scene and follow the action.

2) Write first, edit later. The important thing is to tell the story. If you spend all your time trying to perfect the first scene or the first line, you'll never get the thing finished. Accept that the first draft will be rough, and press on. You can fix it up later.

3) Show, don't tell. This rule wins no prizes for originality; it's one of the most common pieces of advice given to new writers; and yet, it's still one of the most vital. Too many explanatory sentences can leave a scene flat. Encoding the information in action and dialogue

allows the readers to infer it for themselves. For instance, in this scene taken from my short story "The Bigger The Star, The Faster It Burns", Natalie is worried about her friend Ed, and Alejandro is becoming impatient with her, but rather than state either of those facts outright, I communicate them through the things characters say and do:

"I feel kind of bad about Ed," she says. "I shouldn't have left him like that."

Alejandro rubs a sleepy palm across his face. Although bare-chested, he's still wearing his jeans, and his hair's flattened on one side, damp with sweat.

"You don't have to worry about him anymore," he says. "You have me now." He lights a cigarette from the pack on the bedside table. Natalie sits up and hugs her knees.

"Do you think he'll be all right?" There are steel drums playing in the street. She gets up and pulls back the net curtain, looks down at the crowd. She says: "It was just a stupid argument."

Her shoes are lying on the floor by the door. In the orange half-light, Alejandro holds the cigarette pinched between his thumb and forefinger. He takes a small, tight drag and curses in Portuguese.

"Come to bed," he says.

4) Use small details to suggest the bigger picture. Describing each and every character and setting in meticulous detail isn't always possible, or desirable, and

to do so will severely hamper the pace of the story you are trying to tell. Better to pick a few telling details which suggest the rest – as in this example, also taken from "The Bigger The Star, The Faster It Burns", in which we first meet Natalie and I use half a dozen small details to give you the sense of her as a whole person.

Ed stops at a lonely roadside café on a hot autumn night. He drums his fingers on the counter.

"Hey, how about a coffee?" he says. It's late and he's the only customer. The waitress comes over. She's eighteen or nineteen, with long hair and black eyeliner.

"I'm waiting for the water to heat up," she says. She's got a black t-shirt and there's a biro behind her right ear. She looks over Ed's shoulder. "Is that your car?"

He turns in his seat. He's left the Dodge across two handicapped spaces in the empty car park.

"Isn't it a beauty?" he says.

She looks at the sweeping tailfins and scratches her chin. There's dried egg on her sleeve.

"It looks old," she says. "Is it American?"

5) Make use of all five senses. Our senses have a powerful connection to our memories and imaginations, and invoking them can really bring a scene to life in the reader's mind.

It's midnight. Ed opens his door and climbs out, camera in hand. He can smell the heather. He walks over to the nearest fragment. The metal's smooth and warm to the touch. With a dry mouth and sweaty palms, he starts snapping; knowing the pictures he's taking will make his reputation.

Back in the car, Natalie lights a cigarette. She puts her feet up on the dashboard and lets her long hair fall over the back of the seat. She knows there are armed helicopters patrolling the main crash site to the north. But here in the valley, all she can hear is the click of Ed's camera in the hot night air.

> # Go out and have as many experiences as you can. Live, love, laugh. Listen to the way they talk. Find the thing that makes them tick. The thing that drives them. Rage, guilt, insecurity, pride... Everything else follows from there.

3 Ways Of Finding More Time To Write

One of the questions people often ask me is: "Where do you find the time to write?" When they ask this, I often think that what they really mean is: "Why can't I find enough time to write?"

From personal experience, I know how difficult it can be to find the time and energy to be creative, especially if you have a full time day job, a mortgage to pay, and a family to look after, and I won't pretend I have all the answers. But there are strategies you can use to increase the time you have available for writing. The three strategies listed below have worked for me, or for other writers I know personally.

1. Squeeze It In

Think of all the time you spend waiting for things. Can you snatch a few minutes while waiting for the morning bus? Can you sit down at the kitchen table while waiting for the kids' lunch to finish cooking? If you keep a notebook and pen with you at all times, you can turn any period of inactivity into a short burst of writing. If you have a lunch hour at work, why not eat your sandwich at your desk and spend the hour writing? Stuck in the dentist's waiting room for half an hour? That's half an hour you could use to work on your next scene. It may not seem like much, but it soon adds up, and every sentence you write is one sentence closer to a finished manuscript.

Example: My brother wrote the majority of his first novel on the train to work, thereby converting the daily commute into a daily creative writing session.

2. Make The Most Of What You Have

If you already have some time set aside for writing, are you making the most of it? Or do you sit down at the keyboard, exhausted and wondering where to start? Do you spend most of you allocated time fiddling around and answering emails, only to have to stop just when the creative juices are starting to flow? If so, you need to make the most of your time, and the key to that is preparation. You need to know what you're going to write before you sit down at the keyboard, and so you need to train your brain to think about your story during the day. If you're subconsciously mulling over the plot of your story while washing the dishes, walking the dog, or doing the shopping, you'll find yourself coming up with all sorts of connections and ideas that you just can't wait to get down on paper. Some of my best story ideas have come while I was in the shower, driving long distance, or walking to the pub. Keep a notebook with you, and you can jot down notes that will have you ready and raring to go when the time finally comes for you to write.

Example: I write notes for my articles or ideas during my lunch break at work, so I'm be ready to start typing them up as soon as I get home to the computer.

3. Creating Time

This is the most radical of the three solutions. If you've tried the two approaches listed above and you still find you're short of time, you need to start freeing up chunks of time that are currently monopolised by other activities. Make yourself a spreadsheet and use it to break the week down into fifteen-minute chunks. Now fill in all the activities you perform over the course of a regular week. How much time do you spend watching TV or surfing the Internet? How long do you spend reading the newspaper or taking a 20-minute bath when a 5-minute shower would be just as effective? Once you have all your activities mapped out, you'll start to see places where you can shave off some time. Do you really need to lie in bed until 11 am on Sunday morning? Can you save time by doing your grocery shopping online in the evening instead of wasting most of Saturday morning fighting your way around the supermarket? Maybe you could let the housework slide a little, or quit your full-time job in favour of something part-time?

Example: I do most some of my writing in the evening instead of watching TV, and I tend to go to bed later than I should, which means I'm usually tired during the day. Sacrificing sleep for productivity probably isn't a wise and sustainable strategy, but it's been working for me for the last few years, and having a patient and understanding spouse is certainly a big help.

At the end of the day, if writing is really important to you, you will find time to do it. But if you simply can't bear to give up watching one of the latest series or going to the pub every night, maybe writing just isn't for you.

Never confuse setting with plot. A rich and detailed background is nothing without rich and detailed characters interacting within it.

Balancing writing with your day job

Unless you're fortunate enough to be independently wealthy, you're probably going to have to get some form of day job to support your writing efforts. But what kind of job best suits a writer, and how do you balance its demands with the demands of your creative life?

Part-time

You may consider part-time work, in order to have as much free time as possible to devote to your next novel. But can you afford to work part time, or do you have a mortgage and four kids to support?

Freelance

You may decide to try working freelance, but beware: finding clients and completing projects will eat into your free time and, if you're not careful, you may find yourself working longer hours than you would in an office.

Full-time

A full-time job will probably pay better than part-time or freelance, and it'll come with better benefits, such as health insurance and a pension. The regular salary will pay your bills and mean you won't have to rely on your writing in order to make money, thereby taking some of the pressure off and giving you time to rewrite and edit your stories until you're 100% happy with them, rather than rushing them out of the door because you're desperate for whatever income they can generate. On the downside, long hours and a daily commute leave little time for actual writing, and if you want to start racking up serious word counts you may have to give up little luxuries such as watching TV and sleeping.

Level of engagement

Do you take a repetitive manual job that bores the pants off you, giving you time to think about your writing; or one that challenges you but leaves you too exhausted to pick up a pen in the evenings? Somehow, you need to find a balance. A boring job quickly becomes soul destroying, whereas a demanding job will drain your energy and creativity.

Some dos and don'ts

Assuming you find the right day job for your needs, you're still going to have to find ways to juggle its demands with your desire to write. To help you, I present this list of dos and don'ts:

• **Don't write at work** unless you're really sure you can get away with it. And if you do, don't use the PC on your office desk. Don't leave any traces of your extracurricular activity. Getting paid while you write may seem like a win-win situation, but its hard to mask the drop in productivity and concentration that will result; and if you get caught printing out your 400 page opus on the company's printer, you're going to find yourself in a whole heap of trouble.

• **Do keep the story ticking over in the back of your mind.** Think about it on the bus, or while you're waiting for the photocopier. Let your unconscious mind pick away at the plot while your conscious mind gets on with putting bread on the table. Many writers will tell you that they have their best ideas while busy doing other things.

• **Do keep a notebook handy.** Keep one in your pocket or bag. If you have a sudden flash of inspiration, you can jot it down. If you hear a snatch of dialogue on the Tube, or want to record the way the sun shines in through the office window, you can scribble it down in note form and write it up properly in your lunch break.

• **Don't try to do too much.** Accept the fact that you'll be tired when you come home from work. Make sure you factor in some relaxation time, or you're going to get too tired and your writing and work will both end up suffering. Not to mention your health.

• **Do keep plugging away.** Stick to it and you'll get there eventually. If you have a dream, work hard at it each and every day. Take small, positive steps. Don't end up as one of those people who look back in later life and wish they'd tried harder.

The point of writing is to add to the sum total of human creation and culture; to communicate the truth about the human condition; to promote empathy and understanding, and expand the collective imagination.

If you don't like a book or a movie, don't waste time griping about it online. Put that anger to good use. Sit your ass down and write the kind of books you want to read; learn how to make the kind of movies you want to see.

Don't hate, CREATE!

5 lessons writers can learn from athletes

While the careers of your average writer and average athlete may seem to have little in common, there are some lessons writers can learn from the way athletes approach their sports.

1. Get Fit:

Whatever their event, athletes maintain a general level of fitness that ensures their bodies are at the peak of health and performance. Similarly, as a writer, you need to take care of yourself on a physical level. Spending all day in a chair, hunched over a keyboard, can be desperately bad for your long-term health. In order to perform to the best of your abilities, you have to make time for a little exercise, even if it's just a stroll around the block. You have to reconnect to the physical world, because it does you good to get out and about; it gives your mind time away from your work-in-progress, and it can use that time to replenish its imaginative energy. Personally, I find inspiration often strikes while I'm swimming or walking. Plus, exercise always puts me in a better mood. I find it alleviates anxiety, depression and stress, which can only be a good thing. If you want to do your best work, you have to be healthy in both mind and body.

[As a side note: at the turn of the Millennium, I gave up both caffeine and nicotine, and my productivity soared. I don't want to get all preachy about your favourite vices (after all, I still enjoy a drink); but I think it's worth noting that you can get a lot more done when you're not preoccupied with watching the clock, waiting for your next hit.]

2. Set goals:

Decide what you want to do and focus on your goal. Visualise the finishing line, whether it's the end of a short story, a novel, or the end of a trilogy, and keep that prize in mind. Don't get distracted by other projects. Focus your energy and attention on reaching your goal.

3.Prepare:

Just as you can't expect to be able to run a marathon without having trained for it, you also can't expect to sit down and hammer out a masterpiece without having done some of the groundwork beforehand. Writing takes mental preparation. You have to know how to structure sentences and paragraphs; how to pace your story; and how to write engagingly. You have to practice every day to hone your abilities, and you have to read a lot. You have to read widely, and also within your chosen genre. In training, athletes subject their own performance, and the performances of their competitors, to careful, critical study. You need to do the same with everything you read and write.

4. Think globally:

Whether it's football, athletics or swimming, most sports take place on a global stage, with players from all countries and faiths competing. We live in a diverse, globally-connected society, and there seems to be no sign of that trend diminishing in the future. Science fiction that revolves purely around white, middle class Americans in space seems dated and parochial now. It's no longer enough to write comfortable Western-centric yarns of American manifest destiny writ large. The world has changed, is changing, and will continue to change. The models that served us in the 1960s and 1970s no longer apply. I'm not suggesting that you should resort to using characters of other faiths and nationalities as "tokens" in your writing; just that if you want to reflect the world as it is, you should think very carefully before restricting yourself.

5. Go hard or go home:

If you're not writing to the best of your abilities, you're wasting your time. Every story you write should be better than the one before. Be ambitious. Dare to fail. Push yourself to the ragged edge of your abilities and see how far and how fast you can go. Because, if you won't give it all you've got, what's the point of doing it at all?

At the end of the day (to use a sporting cliché), you have selected your arena, and it's up to you to give the best performance you possibly can. And in order to do so, you need to prepare and work at it.

Some writers misunderstand the phrase, "kill your darlings". It doesn't mean you *have* to delete the parts of your work of which you're proudest; it simply means you must be prepared to do so *if it becomes necessary*.

Otherwise, let them breathe. Let them fly. Keep them and ditch the rest. Chances are, they're your real voice.

A simple trick to keep your creativity flowing

If you're writing a novel, there's a little trick I've found useful.

When I come to the end of a chapter, which coincides with the end of my writing time. I generally feel pretty pleased with how it went, and feel I've achieved something by finishing the chapter. I could save the document there and then, and go off to do all the other things I do with my time when I'm not writing. But I don't. Instead, I force myself to write the first sentence of the following chapter before I close Word down for the day.

Why?

Because I find that, rather than starting a new scene from cold, it's easier to come back to a piece that's already in progress. If I leave the manuscript at the end of that chapter, then the day after I'd be facing an empty white page, and I'd have to come up with an opening sentence before I could dive into the action. And for some reason that's far more daunting than simply continuing a chapter that's already in progress.

I might not know exactly what's going to happen in the new chapter, but I do know that I can dive straight into it the day after, without worrying where or how to start – because I've done that already.

Not leaving the book until I've written the first sentence of the next scene or chapter makes it easier for me to pick up next time – a simple trick, but one that keeps the work flowing from day to day.

> # If you want people to read what you write, write about people.

Saving what you take out

When working on a piece of fiction, it is not uncommon for me to decide that a particular scene isn't working, or that the plot should be going in a different direction. When that happens, I have to remove some or all of the material from the manuscript.

But what happens if I later change my mind, or decide that a particular phrase or description can be salvaged for use elsewhere?

For every novel I've written, I've created a file called "Cuts" – a Word document into which I cut-and-paste the bits and pieces I remove from the main story. This keeps all the discarded fragments in one place, making them easy to find, without the necessity to hunt back through earlier drafts in order to locate them.

> I want every story I write to be better than the last one. It's a process. I am always learning.

3 Things To Remember When Writing Action Scenes

When writing action scenes, it can become easy to get bogged down in extraneous detail at the expense of pacing. *Ack-Ack Macaque* (and its two sequels) featured a lot of fights, from fisticuffs to full-blown battles. There was even a dogfight between a WWII Spitfire and a modern Predator drone. When I sat down to write those scenes, I kept the following in mind:

1). Choose the best point of view.

Your reader will be viewing the conflict through the eyes of your characters. Therefore it's vital to choose the right characters. It's no good choosing someone who gets knocked out in the first fifteen seconds, or who spends the entire scene wandering around staring at their feet. Work out what it is you want to show, and then choose the character best placed to witness it – and ideally the character with potentially the most to lose from the ordeal.

For example, in *Ack-Ack Macaque*, I wanted to show the monkey cutting a swathe through a squad of marines. So I chose Victoria's point of view. Frightened and expecting to be shot at any moment, she looks up to see the marines being torn asunder by... something. The adrenalin in her bloodstream slows her perception, and she sees the machete whirling, the gun firing, and we get to share her sense of horrified admiration as Ack-Ack rips through the soldiers.

2). The fog of war.

I've been in one or two semi-serious fights in my life. I've also taken part in several paintball matches – enough to know that when you're on the ground, trying to shoot the guy in front of you before he shoots you, you don't have much of a sense of what's happening around you. Everything moves too fast for you to get a strategic overview of the battle. Rather, you get a heightened awareness of your immediate surroundings. You feel your heart in your chest, the air in your lungs. The smell of the earth and the plants around you. The *pap pap pap* of pellets passing through the undergrowth. Your enemies are flickering figures some distance away through the trees, never clearly glimpsed.

Concentrate on what your character sees and hears and feels. Let the epic sweep of the battle take care of itself. Nine times out of ten, they won't even know if their side's won until it's over. The best way to immerse your reader in the fight is to focus entirely on the specific impressions of your viewpoint character.

3). Keep it simple, stupid.

Unless the peculiarities of your protagonist's gun have a

specific affect on the outcome of the battle, don't bother going into them now (and if they do, you probably should have embedded that information in an earlier scene, to prime us). There's no place here for digressions; we're writing *action* here.

Similarly, don't burden the character with a verbose internal dialogue. If they really have to remember their childhood on a peaceful dairy farm up in the mountains, better they do it before or after the fight. Believe me, when the fists start flying at your face, there isn't time to think of anything else. We've read comics where superheroes have time to trade insults and plot explanations between punches, but in reality, that's not so likely. Keep the chatter to a minimum. Keep the description focused on what is actually happening, and use short, crisp sentences to keep the action moving.

As an illustration of the above points, this example is taken from my short story, "The New Ships", which appeared in the anthology *Further Conflicts* from NewCon Press (2011).

Bullets zipped past her. She hit the car and slid across the bonnet, landing in a heap on the far side of the crash barrier. Bullets spanged off the old Ford's bodywork. A window shattered.

"Get out of there, Max."

"The door's stuck!"

"Use the window."

She fumbled a second magazine into her gun and got to her knees. She sent a couple of shots in the direction of each chopper. Masked troops were spilling out of both machines. She hit at least one of them, and the others dropped to the ground. Max's head and shoulders appeared through the car window. She grabbed the collar of his plaid shirt and pulled, and they both fell sprawling into the gravel between the crash barrier and the concrete bridge support.

"Keep down," she hissed.

She blinked up her Lens's IM function and sent a pre-prepared SOS to an anonymous orbital inbox.

Max had cut his hands on broken glass. His palms were bleeding.

"They're shooting at us!"

"Help's coming."

She fired a couple more shots. The soldiers were working their way to cover behind the barrier on the central reservation between the carriageways. The car sagged as their answering fire took out its tyres and shattered the remaining windows.

Max had his arms wrapped over his head. Blood dripped from the tips of his fingers.

"They want you alive," Ann said.

He looked up, eyebrows raised. His glasses were scratched. "They do?"

Just as you climb a mountain one step at a time, so you have to keep putting one word after another if you want to finish a book.

A Trilogy of Things I Learned While
Writing A Trilogy

January 2015 saw the UK and US release of *Macaque Attack* from Solaris Books, the third novel in a trilogy that began with the BSFA Award-winning *Ack-Ack Macaque* in 2013, and continued with 2014's *Hive Monkey*. While I had previously written a couple of standalone space operas, these three "monkey books" represented my first complete series, and I learned three main things while writing them.

1. Character arcs

If you're embarking on a multi-book epic, you need to make sure you're writing about some compelling characters. Writing a trilogy is a huge commitment. Each of the books in the 'Macaque' trilogy took six months to write, which meant spending a year and a half of writing time immersed in the same fictional universe, in the company of the same fictional individuals.

And what I learned was this: if you're going to be spending a lot of time – potentially years – in their heads, you have to give them the potential to develop and grow in interesting ways. Otherwise, you're going to get bored of them, and if you do, you can be sure your readers will as well.

In the Macaque books, each of the characters has an arc that runs through the trilogy. For *Ack-Ack Macaque*, the titular simian at the centre of much of the action, that arc is a journey that takes him from loner to family man. He starts off as a traumatised escapee from a laboratory, angry and liable to lash out at the slightest provocation; and ends up (having gradually lowered his defences and allowed friends into his life) older, calmer and wiser. He goes from being indestructible and reckless to mortal and all-too-human, but gains so much along the way. He comes to understand the world, the true cost of his actions, and gathers around him a strange, barely functional "family" of damaged individuals. In this sense, his story is the same one we all go through – of growing up, accumulating responsibilities and scars, and building meaningful relationships.

The other major character, Victoria Valois, is on the opposite journey. At the start of book one, she has lost her husband to a particularly brutal murderer. Through the course of the trilogy, she has to come to terms with this loss – a process made complicated by the presence of his electronic "ghost", a self-aware download of his personality, taken shortly before his death. Her journey is one of shock, denial, grief and vengeance; but at the same time, it is one of empowerment. Through her pain and the situations in which she finds herself, she grows in confidence, ability and self-reliance.

These dual character arcs reflected and illustrated the main themes of the books, and allowed me to significantly change and develop the characters in each volume, creating an ongoing story over and above the main "plot" of each novel. And the response I've had from readers has been fantastic, especially in Victoria's case. A lot of people have been able to identify with her journey from lost and damaged accident victim to self-confident and resourceful badass.

2. Continuity Vs Standalone

With a series, it's sometimes hard to know how much knowledge of previous instalments you should assume on the part of the audience. Will everybody who picks up book three have read books one and two? How much should you recap and explain in order for them to enjoy reading it? And how much can you afford to explain before you start to bore those readers who've stuck with you from the beginning?

While the three books in the Macaque trilogy tell one continuous story, I also wanted to make each of them as accessible as possible to the casual reader. Therefore, each book opens with a short paragraph outlining the origin of the story's world – a timeline where Great Britain and France merges in 1959. Beyond that, each book has its own self-contained adventure, with a beginning, middle and end, and it is the characters that provide the continuity and back story, via dialogue and moments of reflection.

I hope each book can be read and enjoyed on its own terms, but knowledge of the preceding books definitely adds to the understanding and enjoyment of the later volumes.

This is particularly true in Macaque Attack, in which characters from one of my earlier space operas [*The Recollection*, Solaris Books, 2011] make a surprise appearance. You don't need to have read the space opera in order to enjoy the action, but you'll get a lot more out of the story if you have.

3. Each installment needs to change the game

One of the things I was determined not to do was write the same book three times. If this was to be a trilogy, each book needed to add something significant. It had to justify its existence.

After book one introduced the world and brought the characters together, book two needed to turn everything on its head, introducing us to the darker side of our hairy protagonist, and the paths he might otherwise have taken. Then, with book three, I had to take everything up another notch, while simultaneously harking back to the beginning of book one, and the themes that had kicked everything off in the first place.

I had to provide a fitting conclusion while simultaneously tying up all the loose ends from books one and two, and bringing each character's emotional and developmental journeys to a satisfying close.

To Recap:

1. Characters need to be strong enough to carry the weight of the story and hold the attention of the reader. They have to be characters we want to follow and find out more about.

2. Decide how accessible you want each volume to be for readers new to the series.

3. Each volume of the trilogy has to justify its position. It has to bring something new to the party – a new piece of the puzzle, more trouble for our protagonists, something we haven't seen before. Think about the Empire Strikes Back and how it deepened and darkened the Star Wars universe after the bright optimism of A New Hope – every instalment of your trilogy has to similarly turn the tables on the characters and the reader, taking the plot, the tension, the stakes, and the development of the characters themselves, up to a whole other level.

This article originally appeared on Chuck Wendig's Terribleminds website.

Just as the only way
to be a skier is to ski,
so the only way to be a
writer is to write.

Daily Productivity Sheet

To help me make the most of my writing time and achieve my goals, I created a Daily Productivity Sheet in Excel. The idea is that by filling one of these in every day, I'll be able to concentrate on what I need to be doing, and start to feel more positive on a daily basis.

Use this as a template, or design your own. Structuring your day stops you worrying about all the things you need to do, and assigns each its own timeslot, allowing you to concentrate on the task at hand. And by breaking the day down into half-hour slots, it becomes easier to see how you spend your time, and where you could restructure your schedule to include more writing time.

I included space to write your overall goals—such as becoming a bestselling author, losing a stone, or completing a particular novel—in order to remind you of the big picture while you set yourself daily goals, such as a particular word count or number of pages.

Get into the habit of filling-in this sheet each morning, and then using it to review your progress each evening, and you'll soon find it helps you focus on the tasks at hand. Rather than being daunted by the idea of writing an entire novel, you can concentrate on the 500 words you've set as your target for the day. And later, when you look back at previous sheets, you'll be able to see a record of progress, and maybe even spot patterns in your routine that will help you adapt your approach to working in the future.

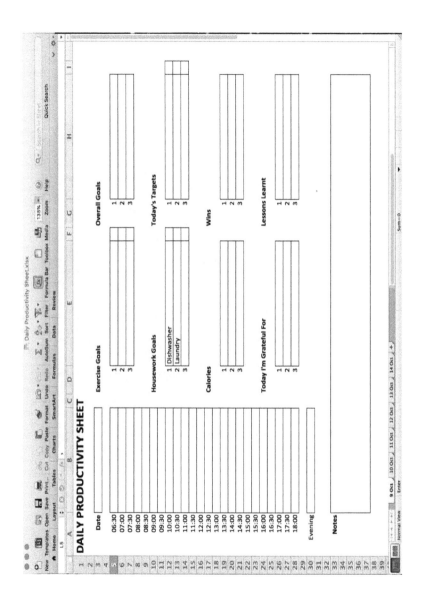

DAILY PRODUCTIVITY SHEET

Date

	Exercise Goals	Overall Goals
06:30		1
07:00		2
07:30		3
08:00		
08:30		
09:00	Housework Goals	Today's Targets
09:30		
10:00	1 Dishwasher	1
10:30	2 Laundry	2
11:00	3	3
11:30		
12:00		
12:30	Calories	Wins
13:00		
13:30	1	1
14:00	2	2
14:30	3	3
15:00		
15:30		
16:00	Today I'm Grateful For	Lessons Learnt
16:30		
17:00	1	1
17:30	2	2
18:00	3	3

Evening

Notes

How do you keep going, month after month? Set yourself a deadline to focus your mind. Pick a finish date, and decide on a treat for finishing on time and a forfeit for missing the deadline. Make a bet with yourself and honour it.

How I Write

When answering questions at conventions and workshops, I'm invariably asked about my routine. People want to know how, where and when I write. Do I do it in coffee shops or at home? Do I use Scrivener or a notebook? Do I write in the mornings or evenings? To help answer those questions, and maybe give some sort of insight into my creative process, I've decided to write this account of a typical working day.

I rise at 6:15 am. I never sleep restfully, so I always struggle awake feeling like something washed-up on a beach. I get out of bed and go downstairs to make my wife a packed lunch. She leaves for work at 6:50 am. Then I feed the cats and make lunches for my daughters. When they leave for school at 8:00 am, I run a hot bath and spend half an hour soaking in bubbles, reading a book. This reading time is important, as it helps my brain ease into fiction mode. It gets the storytelling impulse fired-up, and I often have many of my best ideas while in the bath.

When dressed (I don't work in my pyjamas like some novelists I could mention), I'll fix myself a light breakfast. This morning it was hummus on toast. Then I'll make a cup of tea and be at my keyboard by 9:00 am.

My office is an extension on the back of the house.

It used to be a granny flat, so it has its own toilet and shower. Bookshelves fill one wall. The window looks out at the garden. And my desk – a solid old wooden one that I've had since I was a teenager – rests against the other wall. I keep copies of all my published books beside the computer, to reassure me when I need it that I can write and have written. I keep my BSFA Award on the shelf above the printer for the same reason.

If I've had a brilliant idea in the bath, I'll open Word and start typing immediately. If not, I'll check my email, Twitter and Facebook first. Twitter is important to me because it helps me stay in touch with friends and the latest goings-on and gossip in the industry. It serves the same function for me as an office watercooler. I have various private lists set-up which enable me to quickly check what's happening with industry news feeds, editors and agents, other authors, and booksellers.

The other great thing about Twitter is that it lets me interact with readers. As I work alone at home for most of the day, it's great to get feedback on my work, even if it's just a quick, 'I liked your last book.' It keeps me going on those days when I feel as if I'm shouting into a void.

Tea consumed and Twitter consulted, I then open my current project in Word.

All eight of the novels I've so far written have been composed in Microsoft Word. It suits my way of working. Maybe because I grew up using manual and electric typewriters, I have the screen set to print layout view, so it looks as if I'm typing on a piece of paper.

I do have a copy of Scrivener, which I use when

I'm working on screenplays or comic scripts – I've just never felt comfortable using it to write a novel. I prefer to have the whole thing in front of me and write from start to finish. When I'm working on a book, I feel as if I'm creating a thing. A whole object. Not a bunch of components that will only be compiled together at the end.

I find background sounds helpful while I'm working. Music can be good, but can also be distracting. I used to listen to Brian Eno's ambient albums, but found them too relaxing. Now, I'll either listen to instrumental jazz – such as the album Something Else by Cannonball Adderley, or background noise. There are many YouTube videos offering ambient sounds, but I tend to find coffee shop sounds particularly helpful. For some reason, they help me concentrate and focus on what I'm writing.

Figuring out where ideas come from can be tricky. As I mentioned, I get many of my best ones in the bath, or from dreams. But they don't feel like bolts of lightning from above; it's more like the feeling you get when you slot that final jigsaw piece into place and suddenly you can see the picture you've been putting together for days, weeks or months.

Starting out, I'll know I want to write a particular type of novel – space opera, alternate history, crime thriller – and I'll kick around a few ideas. I'll often start with a half-formed idea. For the first Ack-Ack Macaque book, my initial idea was a murder mystery set on a city-sized airship. I wrote several plot outlines, keeping some bits and ditching others, until I had the vague shape of a story.

I had the essential ingredients – the airships, the dream catcher technology, and the main character investigating the death of their ex, who was being carried around as an electronic ghost in their head.

But it was only when I realised I could slot Ack-Ack into the story that it finally came alive.

And that's how I work.

At one point, when I was trying to write a crime thriller, I went through ten different plot outlines, pruning away the parts I didn't like and keeping the parts I did, until I came up with something that was hugely removed from my initial ideas, but definitely a product of them – the same way a Chihuahua is a product of a wolf. It's an evolution. Each draft of the outline is better adapted than the one that went before. And adaptations that don't work are left behind in favour of new ones, until at last I've created the perfect monster... Mwhahaha!

Sorry. Getting a bit carried away there.

But hopefully you get the gist of what I'm trying to say. For me, coming up with a novel is a two-stage process. First there's the initial idea, then the refinement of that idea.

Ideas and characters accrue until the whole thing achieves a critical mass and sparks into life – and I know I have a story I can write.

Then I send the outline to my agent to see what he thinks, and he'll usually come back with some points I haven't considered. But that's great, because it helps further refine the idea. It makes sure I have the bases covered.

Sometimes, I'll write a few chapters before realising I need to change the outline again. Sometimes these chapters are filed in my archive file, never to see the light of day; and sometimes, I can cannibalise the best parts of them for later drafts.

As to where all these ideas and refinements actually originate... That's the real mystery, isn't it? I guess everything I've ever read, experienced or watched has been filed away in my head somewhere, and occasionally, unexpected connections or associations are made between previously unrelated thoughts.

Sometimes those connections are stupid. But sometimes, as when I absently jotted the words "Ack-Ack" and "Macaque" next to each other in my notebook, they lead to all sorts of unpredictable places.

Around midday, I'll stop to fix myself some lunch. Usually some soup and cheese. I try to stay away from sandwiches, as I find carbs at lunchtime make me drowsy in the afternoon. I eat at my desk while replying to emails and checking social media, then it's back to writing again.

Of course, when I say "writing", I don't mean I'm constantly typing. There's a lot of thinking and research involved. An afternoon of hard thinking might look unproductive from the outside, if judged purely in terms of number of words produced, but can be vital to the overall success of the work-in-progress.

"Writing" can also encompass a host of secondary tasks, such as producing blog posts, responding to interviews; talking via email with my agent, Alexander; editing manuscripts; maintaining my Patreon page;

writing my monthly email newsletter (you are all signed up to that, I hope!); and updating my website.

During the day, the cats provide various levels of company and distraction. One of the kittens is particularly fond of pacing back and forth across the keyboard while I'm trying to type. The older cat sleeps on the sofa in the office, and snores loudly.

Ideally, I'll work through until the kids come home from school at around 3:40 pm. Then I switch back into parental mode and start working on an evening meal.

If I'm feeling particularly inspired, I might come back to the keyboard later in the evening, and often write from 9:00 or 10:00 pm until around midnight. Then I might read for little while before going to sleep.

I mentioned having a lot of good ideas while in the bath. Well, I also have a lot while lying in bed, on the cusp of falling asleep. That's why I keep a notebook and pen beside my bed. I'd hate to lose a good idea because I was too sleepy to get up and write it down. With a notebook on the nightstand, all I have to do is reach out my hand and scribble a couple of sentences.

And that's it. That's how I spend my time. I'm not saying my routine is the best or that it might work for anyone else; if you asked a dozen authors how they spent their working days, I suspect you'd get a dozen different answers. I just hope I've answered your questions and given you a little glimpse behind the curtain.

Don't be disheartened! Writing a book is hard work, but it's worth it. Even if you only write 500 words a day, you will have a 100,000-word manuscript within six months.

Everybody's a geek about something

When I was at school, "geek" was a term of abuse. It was what the cool kids called those of us who were into computers, prog rock, sci-fi and reading. But then all the geeks grew up, started software companies, made movies, and changed the world. And now everybody's a geek, they say. Geek is chic. But that's missing the point.

Yes, we sci-fi kids may have taken the mantle a few years earlier than the rest of you, but you've always been geeks too. A passion is a passion; a hobby a hobby. One hobby can't be called more 'geeky' than another. You can be a football geek, knowing every statistic of your favourite team's last ten seasons. You can be a car geek, able to quote makes, models and performance stats. You can be a Gilbert and Sullivan geek, able to quote any lyric from any of their operas. You can be a real ale geek, able to tell your Parson's Plum from your Whistle Belly Vengeance in a blind taste test. A fashion geek. A music geek.

At this point, "geek" simply means "excited by, and knowledgeable about".

I look at the TV schedules and I see programmes about baking, antique collecting and DIY. Everybody's a geek about something. Embrace your passions, and enjoy them. Get excited by them. Make stuff, bake stuff, collect stuff. Learn how to use a broadsword. Take photos of planes. Take up wine tasting. Just let your fellow humans be equally excited by their obsessions. Be tolerant of each other, and let's recognise the passion and joy our various and varied obsessions bring us, even if we don't share them.

If a scene isn't flowing, try writing the dialogue first. Write the conversation out in real time like a script. You can go back and add in descriptions later. For now, just step back and let the characters interact.

What Is Science Fiction?

In 2016, I gave a talk on science fiction as part of a schools conference organised by the UK Space Agency and the University of York. One of the first things I had to do for my audience (mostly school children and parents) was define what science fiction meant.

The trouble is, genres can be slippery to pin down, and there are almost as many definitions of science fiction as there are critics writing about it.

I started with a slide quoting Isaac Asimov:

> "Modern science fiction is the only form of literature that consistently considers the nature of the changes that face us, the possible consequences, and the possible solutions."

It's a pretty good quote. The "changes" it mentions can be changes in technology, sociology, politics, or biology (among others), and the consequences of those changes can certainly drive a story. Take *Neuromancer* or *The Stars My Destination* as examples. I'm not so sure about solutions, though. Since Asimov's time, science fiction writers seem to have become more wary of offering solutions to the problems they write about. Perhaps life seems more complex now. Perhaps we've lost that post-war optimism and faith in science.

In contrast to Asimov, JG Ballard (writing in his memoir, Miracles Of Life) described his initial reaction to the genre:

> "... science fiction was far closer to reality than the conventional realist novel ... Above all, science fiction had a huge vitality that had bled away from the modernist novel. It was a visionary engine that created a new future with every revolution, a hot rod accelerating away from the reader, propelled by an exotic literary fuel as rich and dangerous as anything that drove the surrealists."

For him, science fiction was a means to stretch and warp reality. It was a tool for examining ourselves. If the business of art was to hold a mirror up to the world, Ballard's idea of science fiction was that of a funhouse mirror, able to distort and exaggerate certain features for narrative, comedic and metaphorical impact.

For me, good science fiction should blow a reader's socks off. It should take that whole cupboard of toys and use it to tell stories that just can't be told within the confines of mainstream literature. And in an increasingly bizarre world, maybe SF is the only literature capable of addressing the things we see on the news every night: cyber warfare; cloning; urban decay; ubiquitous surveillance; global terrorism; encroaching dystopias; etc. Which could be why more and more mainstream writers are finding themselves having to borrow from SF's toy cupboard in order to tell their stories. But more than all that, it should show readers something they've never seen before. It should entertain and stretch their minds, and open them to new possibilities. It should combat prejudice and ignorance. It should educate and provoke and ask the questions no one else is asking, and it should have something to say about what it means to be human in an increasingly baffling world.

Writing in the introduction to William Gibson's Burning Chrome, Bruce Sterling put it like this:

> "If poets are the unacknowledged legislators of the world, science fiction writers are its court jesters. We are Wise Fools who can leap, caper, utter prophecies, and scratch ourselves in public. We can play with Big Ideas because the garish motley of our pulp origins makes us seem harmless. [...] Very few feel obliged to take us seriously, yet our ideas permeate the culture, bubbling along invisibly, like background radiation."

Maybe because of this ability to seem "harmless", science fiction also has a secret history of protest. Soviet writers snuck subversive ideas into their science fiction, and writers in the US and UK have long used the genre to air critiques and grievances.

Historically, science fiction has been the literature of subversion and defiance; and as our world continues to change, it will doubtless be again.

"We will need writers who can remember freedom. Poets, visionaries—the realists of a larger reality."

Ursula K Le Guin

Science fiction shows us other worlds: worlds for us to fear, and worlds to which we can aspire. It can entertain, provoke and infuriate. In the past, it has been dubbed the "literature of ideas", but it is more than that; it is the literature of humanity interacting with itself, its inventions, and the wider expanses of time and space. In short, it chronicles our struggle to understand why we're here, why things are as they are, and how those things might change.

Which brings me back to Asimov's quote.

Definitions are difficult, and rarely encompass everything they set out to define. Sometimes the only way to find out what a genre is, is to write it. If you want to see whether my work measures up to the definitions above, take a look at my books.

Actions have consequences. A stone thrown into a pool creates ripples. In novels, these ripples are the beginnings of our plot.

World Building

World building is a term you often hear bandied about in relation to science fiction and fantasy, but it can easily apply to other genres, from westerns to historical detective fiction. Put simply, it is the process through which you determine the framework of your novel's reality. Not just the backdrop against which your characters act, but also the rules that govern those actions.

If you're setting your story in the contemporary world, you might feel much of your world building has already been done for you. After all, you only need look out the window to see how people act and dress. But what happens if you want to include a vampire character? Suddenly, you have to start considering where this character came from, how it came to be, and how vampires and humans have coexisted up until this point in time. You have to decide what rules the vampires will follow—are they allergic to sunlight and crosses? Can they set foot in a church? Do they glower or sparkle? In short, you're building a world.

With science fiction and fantasy, the term 'world building' takes on a slightly more literal aspect, as often the author has to invent not only his or her characters, but also the very ground upon which they walk. In fantasies such as *Game of Thrones*, this can involve the creation of a detailed map of this new world, along with the different flora and fauna found their, the varying factions and races, and a long, rich history that explains the current geopolitical situation—not to mention a good idea of how the economy works and who grows the food. And that's before we even get into the realms of magic, and the different rules we'll need to invent to constrain its use and prevent every problem in the novel from being instantly fixed by a kindly wizard.

When writing science fiction set on other planets, we must not only invent the planet itself, and decide how its atmosphere is produced, how its orbit affects its seasons, and how the gravity affects its inhabitants—we must also decide how our characters got there in the first place. If humans are moving from one planet to another, we need to know how their starships work, because it will have a profound effect on the events of the story we're trying to tell.

For instance, deciding if our spaceships can fly faster than the speed of light dictates the timescale of our story. If we obey the currently accepted laws of physics, it's likely our heroes will have to enter some form of cryogenic sleep in order to prevent them dying of old age before they reach their destination. But if you'd prefer for narrative reasons to move your characters from one place to another on a scale of days or weeks rather than centuries, you're going to have to invent some kind of faster-than-light drive. But, just as fantasy writers have to invent rules and limitations for the way magic works in their worlds, so SF authors have to work out guidelines for the ways their spaceships behave.

Luckily, we don't have to know exactly how our starship's jump drives actually work (if we did, NASA would be showering us with money right now), any more than we have to know actual magic spells in order to write about magic. But what we do need to know are the limitations involved. After all, when writing a western, you would know a horse couldn't carry its rider from Tombstone to New York in the course of a single day, and you would know the number of bullets in the hero's revolver, and that he or she couldn't mow down an entire army of bandits without having to pause and reload now and again.

In my most recent novel, *Embers of War*, I postulate 'higher dimensions' in which the usual laws of physics are mutable and the speed of light can be exceeded. I liken the process to a dolphin leaping out of the water into the air. For a moment, the dolphin finds itself moving through a different medium, where it moves faster because the water no longer drags on it. However, in order to give my characters time to interact and get to know each other, I've had to impose a speed limit on hyperspace travel. It can't be instantaneous, and journeys can take days or weeks, and regular fuel stops need to be made to keep the engines powering the ships forward.

Whatever you decide, the way your starships move, your vampires evolve, or your magic operates will shape your story, for good or ill. But learning to live within the limitations you impose will help make your story more interesting and authentic, and give your characters more obstacles to overcome.

Ask 'what if' questions. Try to ask questions no one else is asking. Use genre as a delivery system for the story, not as an ends in itself. Smash seemingly unrelated ideas together to see what happens. Speak with your own voice.

Seven Books That Changed My World

Some books change the world. Read at the right time, they have the power to change our thinking, to inspire us, and to change our lives. When we put them down, we are no longer the same people we were when we picked them up.

The books listed below are the books that have had the greatest impact on my life and my development as a writer. I'm not claiming that they're the best books ever written (that's a topic for a different article); but each holds a special place in my heart, and each has contributed something to the way I now see my relationship with the world around me. Although some of them have aged badly, if I hadn't read them when I did, I wouldn't be the same person I am today.

Some books change the world; and these are the books that changed mine.

1. *Of Time And Stars* by Arthur C. Clarke

I found this book in the school library at the age of eleven. It was the first adult science fiction I'd ever come across. Up until that point, I'd been reading books aimed at children, such as Brian Earnshaw's Dragonfall 5 series for younger readers, which used their otherworldly settings as backdrops for rollicking adventures. The stories in *Of*

Time And Stars were different.

A lot of people talk about science fiction having a "sense of wonder". The stories in *Of Time And Stars* blew into my brain like a whirlwind. To this day, I can still remember the awe I felt as I read "The Nine Billion Names of God", "If I Forget Thee O Earth", "All the Time in the World", and "The Sentinel".

Sitting there in my school uniform, clutching the paperback, I felt my mind expand and the scope of my imagination widen. Suddenly I knew that it was possible to articulate strange philosophical questions; that ideas could be communicated through fiction; and that the world was larger and more outlandish than I could possibly have hoped.

I only read the book once, but it was an important turning point for me; it was my own personal Damascus moment, and it set me firmly on the path that would eventually lead to me writing my own science fiction. It opened the door of my imagination and showed me wonders, and I was never quite the same after that.

2. *Biggles Of The Camel Squadron* by Captain W.E. Johns

At about the same time I read *Of Time And Stars*, I discovered this collection of short stories set among the pilots of the Royal Flying Corps, stationed in France in the latter years of World War One.

In those days, there was no radar and no radio either, and a pilot had to survive on his wits alone, with no help from the ground. But this very isolation also afforded pilots great freedom, and as a pilot himself, Johns does a good job of describing the beauty of the French countryside and the exhilaration of flight. But despite this lyricism, the horrors of conflict are never far away and Johns does his best not to romanticise the War.

All that aside, the thing that really makes these stories stand out from the usual "Boys Own" fare is the character of Biggles himself. He's a practical man with a deep-seated sense of sportsmanship and fair play. Sometimes he exhibits great energy and enthusiasm; other times, a profound world-weariness. He's brave and quick to anger, but he's also reluctant to place himself in unnecessary danger, and he prefers to outwit his enemies rather than slaughter them.

Biggles taught me that heroes can think their way out of situations, using their intelligence rather than their brawn. When confronted with problems, they can pause to carefully consider a response, rather than simply diving in with all guns blazing.

The main character takes a similar approach in Robert Heinlein's young adult novel *Have Spacesuit, Will Travel*. In both books, the emphasis is on problem solving and survival, rather than needless heroics.

Also recommended are Johns' other two WWI collections: *Biggles of 266* and *Biggles Pioneer Air Fighter*. Although Biggles' career saw him still flying in WWII and beyond, these early stories rank among his very best.

3. *The Ringworld Engineers* by Larry Niven

As a teenager, this was probably my favourite book. I discovered it at my local library and must have read it at least a dozen times. It took the sense of wonder I'd found in Clarke's stories and magnified it a thousand-fold. Its pages were filled with beautiful vampires, flying cities, carnivorous sunflowers, ancient libraries, and dangerous aliens; and all the action took place on a hoop encircling a sun, with a surface area a trillion times that of the Earth.

In Louis Wu, Niven had also created a self-reliant, intellectual hero in the Biggles mould. Instead of violence, Louis used tools, reason and deduction to overcome the seemingly insurmountable problems facing him. To him, the whole world was a puzzle to be solved. Given enough time, there wasn't anything he couldn't figure out.

This book literally changed the way I thought about the world. It rekindled my fascination with science and learning, and prompted me to really start questioning the workings of everything I saw around me.

After reading *The Ringworld Engineers*, I devoured the rest of the books in Niven's "Known Space" series, including the stories of the albino space pilot Beowulf Shaeffer, which were a direct influence on *A Long Way From Home*, the first proper short story I ever wrote, and the first one I typed on a typewriter.

In February 1988, Diana Wynne Jones reviewed *A Long Way From Home* as part of a local arts initiative to encourage young writers, and talked me through her comments over a cup of coffee at the Watershed in Bristol. It was the first professional feedback I'd ever received, and contained some invaluable pointers. I still have her handwritten notes and while I can't recall the exact words she said, I do remember coming away from the meeting filled with resolve and determined to write science fiction.

4. *On The Road* by Jack Kerouac

I first read On The Road at the age of seventeen, a few months after meeting Diana Wynne Jones, and for a while it ruined all other books for me. It's a vast, sprawling epic and a masterpiece of compelling narration, and I still rate it as my number one favourite book of all time. Every time I read it I see something new, and I'm struck again by the rhythm and poetry of the language, and the immediacy of Kerouac's descriptions. When he writes about sleeping on a hot car roof in the sticky jungle, and the soft rain of bugs falling on his skin, you're right there with him.

I think Kerouac's a very misunderstood writer. People get caught up with the beatnik craziness, and they miss the sadness at the heart of the book: the unspeakable, inescapable loneliness of the American night.

I followed *On The Road* with a selection of Kerouac's other works, such as *Desolation Angels*, *Big Sur* and *The Dharma Bums* – which in turn led to an obsession with the Beat Movement that heavily influenced the poetry and fiction I produced during my time studying creative writing and American literature at university. I still haven't completely shaken it off two decades later.

5. *Burning Chrome* by William Gibson

From reading Larry Niven and Arthur C. Clarke, I had this image of the future as a place of utopian technocratic expansion. Sure, there were aliens out there and the human race might get into trouble once in a while, but on the whole we were going to build spaceships, cure disease and death, and expand unstoppably into the galaxy.

Much as I enjoyed reading those stories, I couldn't write them. I tried to write a few in that vein but struggled badly. I just couldn't find anything original to say. It wasn't until I read William Gibson's first collection *Burning Chrome* that I realised there was another way to do it. This book blew my socks off. It took the pristine future I'd been used to and rubbed its nose in the dirt. It took everything down to the level of the street. The characters were flawed, selfish, and greedy, and out for themselves. But, more than that, it was extremely well written, in a pared-down prose that taught me a lot about the value of brevity and narrative focus.

In many ways, *Burning Chrome* had the same effect on me as the Velvet Underground's first album. It managed to simultaneously remake its own genre while still loving and respecting its roots and influences. At that point, I'd read nothing else like it.

It reinvigorated my enthusiasm for science fiction, and led me to discover Bruce Sterling and the rest of the

Cyberpunk movement, as well as Raymond Chandler and Ernest Hemingway. It inspired me to get serious about my writing. Without it, I would never have written the stories in my first collection, *The Last Reef and Other Stories*.

If I had to point to the one book that had the biggest impact on the development of my writing style, it would be this one.

6. *Consider Phlebas* by Iain M. Banks

Consider Phlebas was a gift from a friend, and it continued my re-engagement with science fiction as serious literature. It took everything I liked about the genre and cranked all the dials up to eleven. In terms of scale and action, it makes *Star Wars* looks like a disagreement at a vicarage tea party. There are huge, intelligent spaceships; battles fought in the gloom of underground railway tunnels; desperate fights beneath the whirling blades of liner-sized hovercraft; and city-sized ocean-going ships ploughing into icebergs the size of Europe. And it all takes place against the backdrop of the Culture, a post-scarcity civilisation where nobody goes hungry and everyone has access to anything they need. The characters are as multi-layered, flawed and human as those in any mainstream novel, and even the supporting characters come across as real, three-dimensional people labouring beneath the burdens of the own hopes, dreams and failures. *Consider Phlebas* immediately became something to shoot for, a marker showing what science fiction could be if done properly – epic without being pompous; political without being preachy; and with prose and characters as finely crafted as those in any other branch of literature.

7. *Generation X* by Douglas Coupland

I discovered this book while at university, and it spoke powerfully to me about what it was to be twenty years old in the late 1980s and early 1990s: that sense that all the good musicians were dead, all the good jobs were taken, and that all we really had to look forward to was the threat of nuclear war. Reading it again a few months later, as a graduate working in a call centre temp job, I strongly identified with the main characters (especially Andy and Dag), all of whom have abandoned their "careers" and rejected the consumerist culture they cannot possibly afford, in order to search for some meaning and clarity in their lives. Like them, I detested the wannabe yuppies who thought that wearing a tie and being the supervisor of a telemarketing team somehow made them somebody. I already knew I wanted to be a writer, but didn't know how to go about being one. So I read *Generation X* and dreamed of escape to a simpler life, of moving to the desert and spending my mornings watching the sun rise instead of commuting to a job I neither wanted nor cared about. In the past twenty years, I must have re-read it at least a dozen times, and each time feels as fresh as the first. It feels, in fact, like talking to my younger self.

The only way to write truthfully about your characters is to write truthfully about yourself.

Why I Write Space Opera

While I have been known to write other types of science fiction, there's something about space opera that keeps drawing me back.

"Space opera" has been around since the heyday of the pulp magazines in the 1930s and 1940s. Initially the term was one of derision, likening the genre to tacky "horse opera" westerns. However, just as the hippies and punks of the 1960s and 1970s took their derogatory labels and wore them with pride, so the term "space opera" eventually became a byword for action-packed stories featuring big spaceships and weighty themes.

In terms of reading, I guess you could call it my first and truest love. As a youngster, I discovered Brian Earnshaw's books about the tramp freighter Dragonfall 5 and her crew, and Hugh Walters' UNEXA series about an international team of astronauts. As I got older, I read everything the local library had by Arthur C. Clarke, Robert Heinlein and Larry Niven. Much later, I fell in love with the "New Space Opera" boom of the 1990s, especially Iain M. Banks' "Culture" books, and novels by Alastair Reynolds, Vernor Vinge and M. John Harrison. I discovered older books by Samuel R Delany and Alfred Bester. And recently, I've been awed by Ann Leckie's Ancillary Justice trilogy, and books by Yoon Ha Lee, Adrian Tchaikovsky, James SA Corey and Becky

Chambers.

But what is it that keeps bringing me back to the subgenre? What is it that appeals to me about these tales of exploration and conflict among distant stars?

When I sat down to write *Embers of War*, I decided to throw in everything I loved about space opera. There's a sentient starship with ideas of her own; a jaded captain with a traumatic past; a tough talking space marine, and a multi-limbed alien engineer. There are ancient alien ruins; bizarre twists of physics, and hints of something lurking in the mists of hyperspace.

At its best, space opera contrasts the personal with the cosmic. Human characters struggle against the backdrops of infinite space and deep time, wrestling to uncover the reasons why we're here and what it all means. It gives us a vast canvas on which to make our points. As storytellers, we're no longer confined to one world or one society. If we want to say something meaningful about the world of today, we can let our tales leap from culture to culture, shining a light on our real life existence by showcasing worlds that are very different in almost every respect.

Iain M. Banks was a master at this. In novels such as The Player of Games and Consider Phlebas, he creates opposing political systems in order to show what happens when they collide. And he manages to do it through the medium of engrossing stories about engaging and fallibly human characters.

As a lifelong reader of stories set in space, I knew some of those books would inevitably end up influencing my writing. After all, we're all made up of everything we've ever consumed. So, after much thought, I've prepared the following list of the books I feel had the biggest influence on *Embers of War*.

***Nova* by Samuel Delany** is set a thousand years into the future, and tells the story of Lorq Von Ray, last scion of a powerful and rich dynasty, and his quest to harvest the rare mineral illyrion from the core of an imploding sun. He believes a cargo hold filled with illyrion will be enough to tip the balance of power between Earth and the quasi-independent Pleiades Federation. Operating on several levels, the book explores Von Ray's childhood and current quest, and relates them to Arthurian Grail lore, while also using the literary ambitions of one of its characters to provide a meta-commentary on the process of novel writing itself.

I guess the biggest way *Nova* influenced Embers is the way all its settlements and the interiors of its ships feel second-hand, scuffed and dirty. This isn't a gleaming future, but one where real people live, work, and scratch profanities into the walls of their cabins. The stakes are high, but they're also inextricably bound up in the ambitions and regrets of the novel's protagonist—something that's also very true for the good ship Trouble Dog.

In **Alastair Reynolds' book, *House of Suns***, Abigail Gentian shatters herself into a thousand cloned bodies, and sets out to explore the galaxy. Six million years later, we follow the stories of two of those clones—the lovers Campion and Purslane—as they try to find out why persons unknown have decided to destroy them and all their line. Along the way, we encounter machine people, centaurs, and ancient weapons capable of rending holes in reality itself. If *House of Suns* influenced *Embers of War*, it was in the great sense of freedom the characters felt exploring the galaxy, and the intense, almost symbiotic relationships they have with their starships. Although the ships in *House of Suns* aren't self-aware in any meaningful sense, they are certainly treated as characters in the narrative.

In addition, the decision to name a rescue organisation the House of Reclamation was a deliberate tip-of-the-hat to Alastair, whom I once unsuccessfully invited to work with me on a novel about teams of scavengers breaking into asteroid-like bubble worlds arranged in a Dyson cloud—a setting I eventually used in my 2011 novel, *The Recollection* (Solaris Books).

Next up, we come to *Planetfall* **by Emma Newman**. On the face of it, there's very little crossover between this tale of a traumatised colonist and the most rambunctious goings-on in Embers, but Emma's book really was a key influence. I've known Emma for many years and am honoured to count her as a friend and colleague. When *Planetfall* came out, I read it with eagerness and excitement. It really is a hell of a good book. But its influence on Embers has little to do with its content and more to do with its style. Planetfall is written entirely in the first person, and that was something I'd never tried. So, when I sat down to write Embers, I challenged myself to do likewise.

The final influence I want to mention is **Leviathan Wakes by James SA Corey**. I picked up a copy of this book from the Forbidden Planet store in Shaftesbury Avenue at around the time I had just started writing *Embers of War*. I already knew what I wanted the book to be, but I was unsure if modern publishing still had room for tales of conflict and intrigue among the stars. *Leviathan Wakes* reassured me that it did, and that there was still mileage in tales of tight-knit crews setting out in their trusty old vessels to take on the universe. While it didn't directly influence the content of Embers, it did give me the confidence boost I needed to finish writing it.

These books also demonstrate one of my favourite things about space opera: the same sense of swashbuckling romance you find in novels about pirates—that feeling of freedom and adventure. The idea that all you need is a stout ship and a star to sail her by. My grandfather joined the merchant marines because he loved tales of the sea, and those unexplored reaches of the globe. These days, we have to look a little further afield to find that same sense of venturing into the unknown. Where once sailors would weave tales of distant lands whose inhabitants had four arms, or no heads and faces on their stomachs, now we have to set our sights on other worlds, around other suns. The Earth has grown too small to accommodate the wildness of our imaginations, and journey times too short to truly satisfy our wanderlust.

Like it or loathe it, space opera's always been an

important part of science fiction. Maybe even the heart of the genre. Whatever else may be going on, there have always been books about big spaceships, colossal alien artefacts, and vast interstellar wars.

There's an escapist edge to space opera that's always appealed to me. Maybe I identified too strongly with Han Solo as a child, or maybe it was all those hours playing the Traveller RPG, but there's something about the beaten-up old starship and its roguish captain that pulls me in every time.

Maybe what really appeals is the sense that in space opera, we're all masters of our own destiny. We're not bound by anything, save the need to keep our ship flying and staying one step ahead of our enemies and creditors. We go where we want and we do what we have to in order to survive. And we've seen things you people wouldn't believe. We've left footprints in the multi-coloured sands of a thousand deserts. Our faces have been tanned by the light of stars so far from here their light won't reach this part of space for another hundred years. And we're still questing outwards, still searching for adventure—for an alien invasion to repel or a repressive regime to overthrow.

And, at the end of the day, we get to sit in our ships and look out the windows at the cold, distant stars and somehow make our peace with our place in the unending wonder of it all.

I promote other writers and encourage aspiring authors because I believe those other authors are my colleagues, not my competition. Their success is necessary for mine, in that it keeps the publishing industry alive and keeps people reading books.

THE FEAR

If you want to be a writer, then sooner or later you'll have to face THE FEAR. However confident you may feel as you start to write your latest novel or story, at some point you'll look at what you've written and hold your head in your hands.

"Give up," a little voice will whisper in your head. And that little voice is THE FEAR.

THE FEAR will plant questions and doubts in your head. It will tell you that everything you've ever written is crap. It will tell you that you're not a real writer, and that you should quit now before people find out what a talentless hack you really are and expose you as a fraud.

I have spoken about THE FEAR to other writers, and they all recognise it. They all have that inner demon whispering to them in their darkest moments, undercutting their confidence and self-belief. For some, those dark moments are at the beginning of a project, when they're staring at a blank white page awaiting inspiration. For others, THE FEAR creeps up on them during the editing process, or just prior to submission.

For me, THE FEAR tends to manifest around the halfway point of a novel, when the end seems very far away, and it becomes almost impossible for me to objectively judge whether what I'm writing is any good or not. I start to worry that the characters are jabbering trolls gesticulating their way through a nonsensical plot, and that I'll never reach the final chapter.

If you let it get hold of you, THE FEAR can paralyse you, leaving you unable to function. The only way I've found to fight back is to keep writing; to keep soldiering on until you stagger over the finish line. Only then will you be able to look back with anything resembling objective clarity.

But how do you keep going? How do you keep the motivation going when the voice in your head tells you that you're wasting your time? You can blot out THE FEAR with alcohol, but that's only a temporary solution; and most people find it hard to do their best work when they're smashed.

The only practical way to prevail is to keep your goal in mind. Get in front of your keyboard every day and do the work. Tell yourself that you will finish what you have started. Listen to THE FEAR and learn to identify it. Don't let it trick you. When it starts sowing its seeds, gather them up and lock them in a quiet corner of your mind. Tell yourself: "This is just THE FEAR talking." And try to ignore it. Or, if you can't ignore it, try turning it to your advantage. Harness the nervous energy to make you more productive. Surf that anxiety wave! Tell yourself that you are going to feel THE FEAR, and do it anyway. Keep your eyes on the prize, and keep fighting on until you get there!

A reader will read many books in their lifetime. Just because they read another writer's novel, it does not mean they won't also read yours.

Getting Your Zing Back

Everyday pressures can rob you of your creative spark, and leave you sitting at a keyboard waiting for words that simply will not come. You find you lack inspiration. Nothing you write seems good enough, and all the fun seems to have gone out of it. Some people call this unfortunate state "writer's block"; I call it, losing your zing.

There are many ways to lose your zing: tiredness, stress, overwork, lack of confidence, and depression can each kill it stone dead. But how do you get it back?

Here are seven quick tips to put the bounce back into your writing.

1. Don't panic. Everybody has their off days, and panicking will only make things worse. Try to remain calm and remember: this too shall pass.

2. Stop trying to force it. If you're getting nowhere, stop banging your head against the wall. Trying to force an idea onto the page when you're incapable of doing it justice will only result in disappointment. If you're really stuck, admit it.

3. Get away from the computer. Go for a walk. Get a coffee. Have a nap. Hang out in a library or park for a while. Find somewhere away from your daily routine, where you can relax and forget about everything else for a few minutes. Give yourself permission to relax and to think about other things.

4. Exercise. Go swimming. Mow the lawn. Jog. Exercise stimulates the mind as well as the body, and it makes you feel better. You can't expect to do your best work if you're constantly plagued by the aches and pains that accompany prolonged inactivity. Get the blood pumping and the oxygen flowing, and you'll be able to return to your keyboard feeling invigorated.

5. Read! Remind yourself why you started writing in the first place. Re-read those books you loved, the ones that first lured you into writing stories of your own. Then read something completely unrelated to anything you're trying to write. Give the brain some new food to chew over. Find some new books to inspire you. Immerse yourself in the kind of writing you love to read.

6. Chunk down. Set yourself realistic goals. If writing a whole novel seems too daunting, break it down into smaller tasks. Chunk it down into individual scenes, and concentrate on writing one scene per day. After all, it's much easier (and less scary) to say to yourself, "Today, I will write a scene," rather than, "Today, I will tackle a novel". If you're going to eat an elephant, you have to do it one mouthful at a time. In the same way, you can't write a whole story or novel in one go. Break the narrative up into a series of important incidents, and then write a scene describing each incident.

7. Be a writer. Still lacking confidence? Try to look at the world around you as you would if you were a successful writer. React to things the way you would if you were a successful writer. Let yourself feel the self-confidence. Think yourself into the role until the act becomes the fact.

But, whatever you do, WRITE. Write for fun, write nonsense. Don't worry about publication; take the pressure off yourself. Tell yourself it doesn't matter if it's any good; just scribble something down. You can always go back and edit it later. But, for now, just write whatever comes into your head. Learn to enjoy it again.

Keep calm. Sit down. And write.

I struggle with tidy endings. Life never ends tidily. Instead, I try to lace my endings with possibility. Suggest there's more to come. Because the idea that there's more to come, more life to come for these characters, more for them to do, is the happiest ending I can think of.

What if I never write anything again?

Earlier, I wrote about finishing a trilogy. The part I missed out was the worst part of all: wondering if you *can* write anything else. Indeed, wondering if you will be able to write anything *at all* ever again.

You see, after you've battered your brains against the keyboard for months to produce a coherent (I hope) story, and you've somehow made it work, it's tough and demoralising to go back to the beginning and start all over again.

"Do I have enough left in the tank for another book?" you ask yourself in the dead of night. What if I never come up with another decent idea? What if I've used up all my creativity? What if, when the book I've just written comes out, everybody hates it so much I never get asked to write another? What if I never write another word?

Self-doubt and insecurity are the bane of a creative life. You are only as good as your last book. Every time a new one comes out with your name on the cover, people will use it to judge you and your worth as a writer. And frankly, that can be terrifying – especially if a fundamental part of your self-identity is tied around writing books.

There's only one way to get past it. Only one cure for THE FEAR.

You have to write.

You have to get back on the horse and throw yourself

into another project as soon as possible. Take a little time to recharge the mental batteries, sure. Just don't prevaricate too long, or THE FEAR will start to take hold.

After four novels, I've come to accept that the first 20,000 words of each book will be tough going. It takes a while to ease into the story and for it to take on a momentum of its own. I've come to expect that difficulty and not let it intimidate me.

THE FEAR is a cunning bastard, and adopts many guises.

I will not give in to THE FEAR.

Because, to paraphrase something a wise man once said, I came here to write books and chew gum.

And I'm all out of gum.

Part Three

Getting Out There

Finding an agent

A little while ago, I had a message from a friend-of-a-friend. He had written a book and was asking if I could refer him to an agent. I'm not sure if he wanted me to provide an introduction or simply supply him with contact details, but this is the reply I gave:

I'm afraid I can't open a literary agent's door for you. It doesn't work like that, and agents don't pick books based on referrals. They pick books they love, and books that they think they can sell. My advice to you is:

1) Make sure the book is as good as you can possibly make it, and presented neatly with no mistakes. Also, include a synopsis. Agents want to work with professionals, so your manuscript and synopsis have to look and read like a professional manuscript and synopsis.

2) Do your homework. Buy a copy of the Writers and Artists Yearbook and find an agent who handles the kind of book you have written. Find authors who have written similar books and find out who their agent is.

3) When approaching an agent, go to their website and read their submission guidelines. Some will want

to see three chapters; others will want to see only a synopsis. Some will accept emails; others will insist on postal submissions. Read the guidelines and follow them, or you'll end up in the bin.

4) Keep trying. I got rejected, and other writers I know got rejected many times, before finding an agent. The key is to keep trying, and act professionally at all times.

When writing a synopsis, try to describe the central struggle of the story. Introduce the main character, what they need to overcome and why; how they do it, and how it changes them.

How to write a novel synopsis

Earlier, I wrote about writing a novel outline. Some of that advice applies here, but where an outline is there to guide you as you write your novel, a synopsis is designed to help you *sell* your book.

When I first set out to write my synopsis for *The Recollection*, I found many contradictory articles on the subject. Some said it should be a single page, others that it could be up to ten. The only points they all seemed to agree on were:

- **The synopsis should be written in the present tense.** No matter which tense you use in the book, write the synopsis as if you're commenting on events that are transpiring as you write them: "He goes to the back door and sees the zombies..."

- **The synopsis should be written by an omniscient narrator.** Even if your novel is written from a first person viewpoint, you should still write the synopsis in the third person.

- **The synopsis should tell the prospective publisher (or agent) what happens in the book.** It should be a complete account of the plot, from start to finish, including any twists or denouements.

- **Don't hold anything back and don't try to tease.** If you end your synopsis halfway through the plot, the publisher (or agent) isn't going to be intrigued, they're going to be irritated. This isn't a cover blurb you're writing, it's a book proposal and, in order to judge whether this is a book in which they want to invest their time and effort, the agent (or publisher) needs to get a picture of it in its entirety.

This wasn't much to go on, but it was a start. So, one evening I sat down at my word processor and started writing, trying to turn a box full of scribbled notes and ideas into a coherent narrative outline. I typed out the main points of the plot, using a separate paragraph for each key scene or chapter, and this came to 2500 words and covered just over five pages. To it, I added:

- **A couple of introductory sentences** describing the novel, giving details of its genre and expected length.

- **A 100-word cover blurb.** Like an executive summary on a briefing document, I hoped the inclusion of a blurb at the top of the synopsis would snag the publisher's attention, and give them an idea of how I was envisioning this novel as a commercial product.

- **A bullet-point list of the major themes.** To put the story in context, I included a very short list of the major themes I wanted to address in the book, as some of these wouldn't come across in the simple plot description of the synopsis itself. Not only does this help sell the book as a concept, it also forces you to really consider what it is that your book is *about* – something you really need to know before you try explaining it to anyone else!

- **A short biography** giving details of my previous publications, to show that I had the experience needed to write and complete this book.

- **A bullet-point list of USPs.** Like it or not, publishing is a commercial business, and I had heard stories of other writers having books turned down because the publisher (or agent) thought they were too similar to another book they'd recently handled. To avoid this, I jotted down a list of five Unique Selling Points: five things that (in my opinion) made this book stand out from the competition. These included my particular writing style, and two of the unusual technologies included in the story. I could also have included any relevant life experience or details of any ready-made following that I had.

The final touch was to add my address, phone number

and email to the top of the first page and the bottom of the last.

This left me with a seven-page document of approximately 3,000 words. I submitted it to Solaris Books along with the first fifty pages of the novel and, a couple of months later, the Editor-in-chief came back to say he wanted to commission the book.

Now, I'm not suggesting you slavishly copy my example. The main point I want you to take away from this is that I followed as many rules and conventions as I could find. I wrote the outline in the present tense, from a third person perspective – but I let it be as long as it needed to be in order to get across the main events of the book, and I added my own touches, such as the blurb and the list of themes.

A lot of authors moan about the need to write a synopsis. The thing to remember is that this is YOUR book, and you have to sell both it and yourself. You have to find a way to inject your personality and professionalism into the document.

(But please bear in mind that some editors have very strict guidelines that they want you to follow, so it's worth checking their requirements in advance.)

I'm not saying that what I've described here is the only way to write a synopsis; it's just the way that's worked for me.

At the end of the day, if you have what it takes to be a writer, you should be able to sum up the plot of your novel in a handful of pages. Learning to write a synopsis is just like learning to write short stories or poems: it's another discipline you need to master.

And if (like me) you haven't finished writing the book yet, you'll find the synopsis serves another purpose: you can use it as a plan, keeping you on target as you work towards the final chapter.

Now, get out of here and get typing!

> Watch people when they are angry but don't want to make a scene.
> That kind of tension keeps the pages turning.

A Few Words On Social Media

We live in a connected world, and social media has given readers and writers (and agents, publishers and editors) unprecedented access to each other. When I was a kid, the only way to contact writers whose books I enjoyed was to send a letter to the publisher's address in the book, and hope they passed it on. A reply, if any were forthcoming, might not arrive for weeks or months.

And that's why I dithered before including this chapter. The pace of change moves so swiftly that any advice I give you on specific social media platforms, such as Twitter or Facebook, might seem horribly outdated by the time you read this book. So instead, I'm going to give you a few guiding principles that you can apply whatever sites you use.

1. Choose wisely

You can't realistically expect to keep up profiles on every social media platform. Nobody has time to churn out that amount of interesting content, and interact with that many followers. Take a look and see which platforms your target audience uses (and your target audience may include publishers and other writers), and give that one a try. It may take a while to attract a decent following, but if you post useful and interesting content, you will eventually attract the right people.

2. Protect your good name

The publishing world is large, but it is not infinite, and many of the people who work in it talk to each other. If you act like an argumentative asshole online, you run the risk of alienating the very people with whom you want to work.

Personally, I approach social media the same way I would approach a conversation in a bar. I try to be polite and helpful, and never say anything to (or about) anyone that I wouldn't be prepared to say to him or her in person. Remember: you never know who's listening, and whom they might tell about your behaviour.

In addition, I also try to add value. I try to give my followers a reason to follow me, so I tend to include writing tips, book recommendations, and other items of interest in between the plugs for my own work, and I try to show a genuine interest in the people who follow me, by asking (and answering) questions, and doing what I can to help and inspire them.

Just be the best version of you, and you won't go far wrong.

3. Build a list

Mass marketing your wares via social media is all well and good, but your carefully crafted posts can often get overlooked in someone else's timeline. As far as the

Internet is concerned, we're all just drops in the ocean. So sometimes, it's also good to be able to communicate in a less ephemeral fashion. And that's where email marketing comes in.

A few years ago, I started a monthly email newsletter because I decided it would be a more personal way of interacting with people interested in my work. The advantage of an email is that the person receiving it has opted-in to receive it. They are a self-selected audience, rather than a huge mass of social media followers, and they are interested in what you have to say. As long as you don't abuse trust they've put in you, and you include some useful content along with the shameless self-promotion.

In summary:

- Be interesting
- Be interested
- Give people a reason to want to follow you
- Don't abuse their trust—nobody like a spammer or a blowhard

Never be ashamed of the genre in which you choose to write. As long as your work brings enjoyment to readers, it's no less valid than any other type of literature.
Be proud of your work!

Convention Tips

Conventions are great places to meet editors and agents, to make new friends and keep in touch with all the latest industry gossip. So, I thought this might be a good time to share a few of the tips and hacks I've picked since attending my first convention way back in 2007.

Many of the articles you'll find on the web about conventions tend to concentrate on topics such as networking and pitching books to agents and authors. I figure there's no point in regurgitating the same old advice about meeting people in bars, attending book launch parties in order to work the room, and so on. Instead, I want to talk about some of the nitty-gritty practicalities that first-time attendees might find useful.

1) Breakfast. If the price of your hotel room includes a complimentary breakfast, make sure you're up in time to eat it – especially if it's served buffet-style. Load up your plate with twice as much as you think you'll need, and eat as much of it as you can. With luck, you'll be able to skip lunch – which will save you a considerable amount of money at some conventions, where the hotel food is often way overpriced, giving you more money to spend on a decent evening meal, and beer. Also, egg protein is great for mopping up any alcohol still sloshing around in your system. And bacon cures many ills.

2) On Twitter? If your Twitter handle is something other than your name, try including that on your name badge as well. Many's the time I've been talking to "John Smith" for hours before realising I already knew him as "@robotsmonstersandgrr_75" on Twitter. In addition, following the event's hashtag may lead you to a few room parties or other happenings that you might otherwise have missed.

3) Don't be pushy. Nobody likes an aggressive networker, or a show-off. Yes, you might be at the convention to promote yourself, but learn when to give it a rest, okay? These events are supposed to be fun, remember? Take a few minutes to enjoy yourself.

4) Don't be a wallflower. I've made some excellent friends at conventions. Hanging out with a hotel full of people who like the same sort of stuff you do is a joyous and liberating experience. But if you find mixing with people difficult, see the following section about acting confident in social situations: How To Be More Confident.

5) Don't be a dick. Think twice before starting arguments in the bar, or putting somebody down because they haven't read a certain book, or prefer one type of fantasy to another – or are of a certain sex or sexual persuasion. If you're unpleasant, people will remember you that way. I don't care how important you think you are, once you've acquired a reputation as an ass, it's very hard to shift – and, if you've come here to spend time with people who are into the same stuff as you, you don't want to alienate them by being a tosser. Have a bit of consideration, and treat everyone – including the hotel staff – with politeness and consideration. I shouldn't need to say this, but I've seen a few fledgling authors (who should've known better) acting like arrogant pricks when they really should have been paying attention to the people around them, some of who were editors who may otherwise have been interested in working with them. Remember: politeness costs nothing, but rudeness can cost your credibility, your friends, and your career.

6) Pack tablets. After succumbing to a particularly nasty bug at Eastercon a few years ago, which kept me alone in my room for two days wondering if I was going to die, I'd recommend you slip a few medical supplies into your wash bag. There might not be a chemist anywhere near the hotel, so ensure you're well stocked with painkillers, anti-diarrhoea tablets, indigestion tablets, and anything else you think might conceivably be useful. And always make sure you have plenty of bottled water in your room to swig them down with – as well as to rehydrate when you wake up the morning after the night before.

7) Get some fresh air. Conventions can become hermetically sealed little worlds of their own. Try to get out for some fresh air during the day. Phone home. Catch up with news from the outside world. Take a break. Try to see something of the city beyond the hotel carpark. You'll feel better for it when you dive back into the convention's maelstrom.

8) Above all, have fun. Try new things. Go for dinner with a group of people you've just met. Spend the evening at a room party organised by Hungarian sci-fi fans, swigging pálinka from a plastic cup. Attend every book launch and panel you can. Make new friends; meet up with old ones. Join in. Show people that, under your gruff exterior, you're actually a pretty cool person to hang around with. Because conventions are like a gathering of the tribes. These are your kind of people. They like the same sorts of things as you; they get that whole geek thing. So relax, and have fun. And make sure they're having fun too.

9) Pack some biscuits. Trust me, you're going to feel peckish when you get back to your hotel room at 3am, and room service costs a bomb, so it's always useful to have a packet of digestives, or some peanuts or something, squirrelled away in your suitcase... Especially if you skipped lunch.

10) Share. We're all in this together, so if you've got a hard-won nugget of wisdom about surviving conventions, let's hear it. Drop a comment in your socials, and share it with the rest of us.

Everyone gets rejections. Twelve publishers famously rejected JK Rowling before Bloomsbury decided to take a risk on Harry Potter. Keep writing, keep improving, and enjoy the process.

How To Be More Confident

Like many of the writers I know, I tend to lean towards the more introverted end of the personality spectrum, happier communicating via a keyboard than face-to-face, and comfortable spending long periods by myself, simply writing. But, while social media now makes it possible to network (horrible word) without leaving the comfort of your armchair, the pressure is on for today's writer to promote themselves at conventions, book launches and other literary events.

If, like it used to do for me, the very word "promotion" stirs up the butterflies in your stomach, let me share with you the following techniques I've learned over the years that now help me feel more relaxed and appear more confident in social situations.

1. Shake hands. When meeting someone for the first time, shake hands if you can (I know some people have issues with physical contact). It may seem a bit formal, but it breaks the ice, and makes you seem polite and respectful.

2. Ask questions. There's nothing worse than a writer who drones on about themselves all the time. Instead, start the conversation off by taking an interest in the person you're talking to. Ask how they've been, where they've come from, what they've enjoyed about the event so far, etc. If you show an interest, people will open up and, hopefully, ask a few questions of their own.

3. Eye contact. I know you may be shy, but don't spend the whole conversation staring at your shoes, or looking off into the middle distance. It makes the other person feel like you're not really listening to them. Try to look them in the eye when they're speaking. Be attentive. Don't look as if you'd rather be somewhere else. Eye contact is useful for building rapport and showing your sincerity.

4. Listen. Pay attention to what's being said. Don't spend all your time worrying about what you're going to say next. Listen to the other person. Don't just appear to be interested; actually be interested and, before you know it, you'll be talking away like old friends.

5. Speak clearly, then shut up. When it's your turn to speak, don't mumble. If you're a bit of an introvert, like me, the chances are you're naturally quietly spoken, because you're not used to drawing attention to yourself. Well, forget that. Try to talk audibly and clearly. Don't bellow into the other person's face; just make sure they can hear and understand what you're saying. If you talk confidently, while maintaining eye contact, it will make you feel more self-assured. Don't ramble or bluster, and certainly don't brag. If somebody asks about your work, try to be honest and a little humble. Nobody likes a show-off or a blowhard. Simply give your answer, succinctly and politely, and then leave a pause for the other person to speak.

6. Mind Your Body Language. When chatting, try to stand comfortably with an open posture, and try not to invade the other person's personal space. Crossing your arms or staring at your feet can come across as defensive, so do what you can to seem receptive and interested. Standing at a slight angle to the other person feels less confrontational, and allows you (and them) to glance away from time to time.

Written out like this, these techniques may sound a little clinical and cynical, but they're not. They're just common-sense hints to make you more approachable and self-assured. I've used them myself for years and, after a while, they've become second nature. One day, you'll suddenly realise that, by acting confident, you've actually *become* more confident.

There's no trick to it. If you want to be more self-assured, simply act as if you are, and, eventually, you will be. The feelings will catch up with the behaviour, and you won't find meeting people nearly as nerve-wracking as you used to.

Be ambitious. Dare to fail. Push yourself to the ragged edge of your abilities and see how far and how fast you can go.

A Few Words On Mental Health

I want to say a few words about writing and mental health. When I was younger, I had my own experiences with depression and anxiety, and they went on for years before I realised what they were. At times, I felt like no one could possibly understand what was happening to me. I couldn't even explain it to myself. Was I going mad, or was the world just an unbearably horrible place? It was impossible for me to objectively examine my mental state.

Finally, after a friend opened-up about her anxiety, I was able to put a name to what I felt. But, even then, I resisted getting help. I didn't want to admit my problem out loud for fear of sounding weak or foolish, or becoming unemployable. In other words, I was anxious about what might happen if I admitted to my anxiety. And I worried that medication might rob me of the creative spark that drove my writing. I worried it might somehow make me less sensitive and blunt my muse.

Thankfully, as it turned out, these fears were groundless.

You don't have to be depressed to write well. Your brain is your instrument, and you need to care for it. And that means getting help when you need it. If you feel anxious, paranoid or depressed, get help. Talk to someone. If you don't know who to turn to or confide in, you can talk to charitable organisations, such as the Samaritans, in confidence. But please, talk to somebody. Bottling it all up makes it so much worse.

The good news is, I eventually went to my GP and got the care I needed, and am now in a much better place. So, please take care of yourself, and don't suffer needlessly.

Exercise and fresh air are good. Good food and company help. Try to stay hydrated, go for a walk every now and again, and don't cut yourself off from the world.

> Write a damn good book. Only submit your very best work. Perhaps build a name for yourself through short stories. Always be professional and polite. Keep trying.

My Journey

Everybody's journey to publication is different, but I thought it might be useful to recount my own experience.

I completed the first draft of my first novel (*Silversands*) in 2002. I was 32 yrs old, working a full-time job in software marketing, and about to get married. The book didn't appear in print until 2010, when Pendragon Press published it in limited edition hardcover.

During that time, I wrote lots of short stories. One of them wound up in Interzone, which led to the publication of my first short fiction collection, *The Last Reef*, in 2008, again in a limited print run (300) from a small press.

While those two books only sold 600 copies between them, *Silversands* got positively reviewed in *The Guardian*, and subsequent stories in *Interzone* (including the original 'Ack-Ack Macaque' short story) meant publishers and agents knew who I was. So, when I submitted a novel proposal to Jon Oliver at Solaris Books (after being introduced to him by Lee Harris at a convention), he was wiling to take a punt. I wrote the novel in six months and it came out the following year, 2011, as *The Recollection*.

I'm very fond of *The Recollection*. It attracted some good reviews, but didn't set the world alight. So I wrote another, *Ack-Ack Macaque*, and that one won the 2013 BSFA Award, tying with Ann Leckie's all-conquering *Ancillary Justice*. In fact it was the only other novel to get a look in that year, as *Ancillary Justice* went on to win the Hugo, Nebula, and Arthur C Clarke awards. So sharing that award with her meant some people started taking me more seriously (although the picture of the monkey on the cover meant others took me less seriously. C'est la vie).

Two macaque sequels followed. Then I wrote a novel, *The Uncertainty Principle*, that never quite gelled and I eventually abandoned. Instead, I got a new agent, and we sold *Embers of War* and two sequels to Titan Books. NewCon Press published my second short fiction collection in 2017, nine years after the first, and Embers appeared in Feb 2018, followed a year later by the sequel, *Fleet of Knives*. I also wrote and sold a horror novella, *Ragged Alice*, to the aforementioned Lee Harris at Tor. com... And that brings us up to date. At the time of writing, the final book in the Embers trilogy, *Light Of Impossible Stars*, is scheduled to appear in February 2020.

While all this was going on, I also got married (2003) and raised two kids (born 2004 and 2005). Writing time was scarce, and usually involved staying up late at night. But I stuck with it, despite the low income and late nights. And I'm still sticking with it.

And that's why I've poured everything I learned on that twenty-year journey into this handbook for aspiring authors. I thought I should share what I'd discovered and warn of pitfalls and bumps in the road.

That's also why I do my best to encourage other authors on Twitter. It's a long road for most of us, and we need all the encouragement we can get. And if you've read this far, I love you for it. Go and treat yourself to a biscuit.

Gareth L. Powell
Bristol
July 2018

Next Steps

- Write your own list of 55 story ideas

- Add 100 words to your work-in-progress

- Follow your favourite authors on Twitter

- Recommend this book to your friends

- Experiment with different ways of working. Not all the advice in this book will suit you. Find what works for you

- Work hard, and have fun!

Afterword:

An Open Letter To An Ugly Duckling

Sometimes kids can be cruel. When we're young, we're all thrashing around in the dark trying to figure out who we are and how we're supposed to behave, and that can be very frightening. Unfortunately, some children deal with that fear and insecurity by picking on kids they perceive as being less cool, in an effort to deflect attention from themselves. They try to secure their place in the "in-group" by excluding others.

It's a natural part of life, and a behaviour that probably dates back to our primate ancestors. And it sucks, especially if you are one of the kids being pushed out and excluded.

If I could rewrite the story of "The Ugly Duckling" for you, I'd change the ending.

In the original fairy tale, nobody wants to be friends with the duckling because they don't like the way he looks or talks. Spurned by the world, he takes himself away and hides in the reeds until, one morning, he finds he has morphed into a beautiful swan, and he is immediately accepted by a group of other passing swans.

I can see what this story is trying to say to kids: that you shouldn't worry if you don't fit in, because you might not be a duckling, you might be a cygnet. You might not be beautiful *now*, but don't worry, because you will blossom later in life. All the gangly awkwardness of adolescence will vanish when you've gone through puberty. And then, when you finally look graceful enough, and learn to behave the way we expect you to behave, you will be accepted.

Well, screw that.

Who on earth would want to be accepted on those terms?

In my version of the story, the ugly duckling learns to be comfortable in his own skin. He finds a way to accept himself for who he is. He sets his own goals, and strives for them in his own way. He doesn't care so much what others think of him, and only values the opinions of those who really love and care for him. And instead of finding a group of shallow, prissy swans to take him in, he goes off to university and finds all the other ugly ducklings from all the other villages, and together they realise how cool they really are, and that they don't need--or even want--to be swans.

You see, one thing I learned from school was that it's the geeks, the nerds and the misfits who grow up to be the most interesting people. When you leave school, nobody really cares whether you were good at sports or if you were the most popular girl in the class. None of that shit matters in the real world.

You are not alone.

There are plenty of others out here just like you. They are writing novels and comic books; they are designing computer games and playing in rock bands; they run software businesses, YouTube channels, and record labels; they work in science and engineering, and make art. Somehow, they found a way to turn their nerdy passions into fulfilling and productive lives.

They didn't have to make themselves beautiful in order to be accepted by the world; they were already beautiful and intelligent and strong and interesting.

And so are you.

If you study hard, have a hobby you love, read widely and dream hugely, you will be all right.

In fact, you'll be more than all right. You'll be spectacular.

Acknowledgements

Thanks are due to:

Francesca and Rob at Luna Press Publishing.

My agent, Alexander Cochran at C&W.

Paul Cornell and Cavan Scott, for permission to use their quotes.

All my supporters on Patreon.

My wife Becky and children Edith and Winter, for their constant belief and support.

My parents, Lyn and Roe, for teaching me to read before I started school.

My siblings and fellow novelists, Rebecca and Huw, for long talks and endless encouragement.

My high school English teachers, especially Mark Evans, Lucy Armstrong and Richard Durant.

My friends and colleagues in the writing and publishing community, especially Kim and Del Lakin-Smith, Neil and Gemma Beynon, Adrian Tchaikovsky, Lee Harris, Cath Trechman, Lydia Gittins, Miranda Jewess, Jon

Oliver, Ian Whates, Gillian Redfearn, Stark Holborn, Jonathan Howard, GV Anderson, Aliette de Bodard, and Emma Newman, for comradeship and conversation.

My Twitter followers, for cheering me on.

And finally, Helen Dunmore and Diana Wynne Jones, for taking me out for coffees and offering invaluable advice just when I needed it.